THIS IS A CARLTON BOOK

Text copyright © TWI 2000
Design copyright © Carlton Books Limited 2000

A TWI Production for Carlton © Carlton Television Limited 2000

This edition published by Carlton Books Limited 2010
20 Mortimer Street
London
W1N 7RD

A CIP catalogue for this book is available from the British Library.

ISBN 978 1 84732 404 7

Art direction: Diane Spender
Design: Adam Wright, Michael Spender
Project editor: Camilla MacWhannell
Picture research: Adrian Wood
Production: Lisa French

Printed in China

BRITAIN
AT WAR IN COLOUR

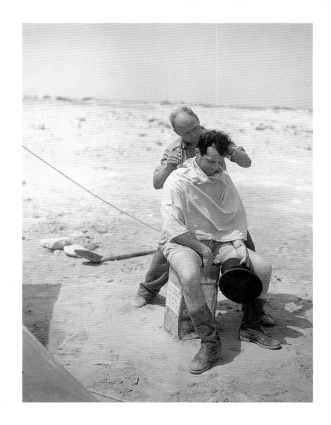

BRITAIN
AT WAR IN COLOUR

CARLTON
BOOKS

STEWART BINNS LUCY CARTER AND ADRIAN WOOD

with Gill Blake, Katie Chadney, Anna Price and Kyla Thorogood

CONTENTS

INTRODUCTION

This book and the ITV series it accompanies, "Britain at War in Colour" are sequels to the highly successful 1999 book and series, "The Second World War in Colour". "Britain at War in Colour" is based on two remarkable treasure troves of historical material: surviving letters and diaries of people who lived through World War Two and rare colour films and photographs of the time, most of which have only recently come to light.

The first television series largely relied on newly discovered films shot in colour by professional cinematographers. About 400 hours were discovered, shot either on the German stock, Gasparcolour, or the American stock, Kodachrome, both developed in the early thirties.

For the new series, much more amateur material has been found. By the end of the 1930s Kodachrome was beginning to be made available to amateur enthusiasts for their home movies. The interest in colour film generated by "The Second World War in Colour" is leading more and more people to find these old amateur films lying in dusty attics, or deep in the vaults of public collections.

Despite the growing market in amateur colour cine film in the 1930s, colour stills photography remained almost exclusively professional until after the war. Therefore, all the colour photographs for this book are either pictures generated by the wartime Ministry of Information, or by the few commercial magazines which were using colour images at the time, like *Picture Post*.

These photographs are very rare, especially before 1940. Colour processing was very expensive, colour film required strong light and was extremely costly to reproduce and print. Most of the small number of colour photographs from the Second World War are rather "stiff", posed portraits and scenes. But for this book we have chosen the most "natural" ones available. Great care has gone into selecting those which show the experience of war and what it was like to live under siege.

Likewise, the letter and diary material compiled for the series and this book has been taken from the millions of words which have survived in private and public collections. There are 5,000 collections of documents devoted to the Second World War in the Imperial War Museum alone.

The letters and diaries are very well written; perhaps the art of writing was thought to be more important then. It was certainly a time when the telephone was hardly used and e-mail wasn't even a figment of the imagination. Many people kept a diary because it was wartime. They clearly thought their fears, hopes and observations should be recorded for posterity, and often used lines like, "I wonder whether anyone will ever read this?" Well someone has and so will many more as a consequence of this book.

CHAPTER I

THE PRELUDE TO WAR

Britain was a confused nation during the 1930s. The decade began with a Labour Government, headed by Ramsay MacDonald as Prime Minister. However, he lacked a clear majority in the House of Commons, having only 288 seats, to the Conservatives' 260 and the Liberals' 59. In August 1931, the Government, in trying to raise funds to continue with high levels of expenditure and unemployment insurance payments, learned that the Federal Reserve Bank in New York would provide a loan only if the Government cut unemployment benefits by 10%.

The economic pressures on the Labour Government flew in the face of its ideological principles. MacDonald felt he should resign his government, but was persuaded to stay at the head of a new National Government, supported by the Conservatives and the Liberals. Orthodox Labour Party members went into opposition with the words "treachery" and "betrayal" heavy in the air. The new government cut public expenditure by £70 million and unemployment benefit by 10%. Many thought that it was the final ignominy of the abandonment of the "land fit for heroes", promised after the First World War.

With the support of the Conservatives, MacDonald won the General Election that followed the crisis. Unrest followed, as the unemployed tried to cope. There were hunger marches and protests, not just by the working classes but also by middle-class sympathizers. Reactionary counter-protests, by right-wing activists like Oswald Mosley's British Union of Fascists, simply exacerbated the situation.

However, compared with the turmoil in Europe, Britain, although "confused", was not in the throes of revolutionary change. Communist Party membership remained under 20,000 up to the Second World War, while the Fascists, although highly visible, remained a small group of extremists, liberally sprinkled with thugs.

The Labour Party was the anchor point for radical thinking and, although ostensibly "betrayed", remained as a voice of "evolutionary" change, rather than destabilizing violence. Similarly, although establishment thinking was imperialist, highly conservative and even racist, it fell short of reacting to pressure for change in a way that would have served to make change even more likely.

For the traditional establishment, the well-to-do and the gentry, the most important thing was that life went on as before; a life of social exclusiveness, gaiety and tradition.

At crucial points during the thirties, Parliament, the press, public meetings and private discussion seemed to create a climate of debate that suggested solutions by consensus, rather than by

A DREARY WINTER'S DAY IN LONDON'S REGENT STREET.

conflict. Perhaps, that was what the National Government of the time was all about – a stable institution that represented the great mass of middle England. Although the running sore of unemployment was still rife in the provinces throughout Britain, "middle England" was enjoying the products of the newly emerging "mass" society. For the middle classes, popular music, fashion, radio and cinema provided entertainment, especially if it smacked of Americana. There were significant areas of growth and new wealth, many providing the products that drove the new demand, like motor cars and "labour-saving" devices for the home.

Britain was also confused about its role in the world. Its imperial past was still evident. The Empire was still the Empire. The Royal Navy was still a massive power across the oceans of the world. But the First World War had extinguished almost all thoughts of wars of adventure and conquest. So much so, that voices like Winston Churchill's, calling for re-armament to protect Britain and the Empire from the growing threats presented by the new ideologies, seemed so bellicose and yet forlorn.

As it became clear that Communism was not a passing fancy and that Fascism presented a major threat in Europe – particularly in Germany, Italy and Spain – British opinion clung to its belief in the avoidance of the slaughter of war. This belief was latterly given the dirty name "appeasement". But, at the time, it seemed considered, moderate and sensible. It took a strong man to fight appeasement in the thirties and an even stronger one to still believe in peace after 1939.

Moderate opinion believed in the League of Nations and the concept of collective security. It only became "appeasement", in the pejorative sense of the word, in the hands of politicians.

When, in December 1935, Foreign Secretary Sir Samuel Hoare "did a deal" with French Premier Pierre Laval, to concede territory to Mussolini in Abyssinia, in order to secure an end to hostilities, it was seen by British opinion as a breach of the idea of nations acting reasonably to ensure collective security. Hoare had to go. Earlier, in 1935, Ramsay MacDonald had been replaced by Stanley Baldwin as leader of the National Government. In the election that followed, two-party politics was restored, with Baldwin's Conservatives winning handsomely. But the Labour Party became the clear and legitimate opposition. The new rivalry between the two would remain latent for ten years, because of the impending war, only to be given expression after the war.

In 1936, a somewhat personal domestic dilemma illustrated the confusion in British life: the Abdication Crisis. Such were the times that had the new King, Edward VIII, who ascended the throne on the death of George V, wanted to keep the woman to whom he was devoted as a mistress, he would have got away with it. The few who knew in the establishment, and those who fawned around them (which in those days included the press), would have said nothing. But Edward wanted to marry Wallis Simpson. Unfortunately, she was an American commoner and, more significantly, already married (for the second time).

The public was told nothing of the problem that was about to confront the nation until after Simpson's divorce was granted. The King put, "love before duty" and abdicated the throne in favour of his brother, who became George VI. Edward became the Duke of Windsor and withdrew to Austria. The crisis was "handled" by the establishment as well as any contemporary "spin doctor" could today. But as a constitutional and moral dilemma for the British people to consider, there had been no debate. The matter was settled as if it were an intrigue at a medieval court.

As the decade wore on, the perfectly laudable prevailing sentiment, inherited in the aftermath of the Great War, to avoid conflict at all costs, began to act against the common interests of European collective security, rather than for it.

Following the crisis in Abyssinia, the Spanish Civil War was the second major threat to European security. Even after appeasing Mussolini over Abyssinia, it was still thought to be expedient not to intervene in Spain. This, despite the fact that both Germany and Hitler were openly supporting Franco's rebels. Abyssinia had been a long way away, although Winston Churchill had argued vociferously that sanctions should be imposed on Italy and that the League of Nations should be encouraged to take firm action. Spain was closer, but here the adversaries were Communists and Fascists. Even Churchill said, "I refuse to become the partisan of either side." He went on, "I will not pretend that, if I had to choose between communism and nazism, I would choose communism. I hope not to be called upon to survive

L–R: PRINCESS MARGARET, QUEEN ELIZABETH, PRINCESS ELIZABETH AND KING GEORGE VI, 1942.

in the world under a government of either of these dispensations. I feel unbounded sorrow and sympathy for the victims."

Churchill had consistently argued against appeasement throughout the thirties and warned in particular about the growing threat posed by Germany. But he had turned sixty and was seen as an ageing maverick. His attempts at support for the King in the Abdication Crisis had further weakened him. Baldwin had kept him from office, and when Chamberlain replaced Baldwin as Prime Minister in 1937, there was still no place for Churchill in the government. Chamberlain believed that it was possible to negotiate with Hitler and that his expansionist plans in Central Europe could be confined to that area only. When Lord Halifax, the Lord Privy Seal, visited Berlin, those impressions were confirmed. In fact, Halifax advocated, in Cabinet meetings, the need to improve relations with Germany.

THE ENTRY OF THE COLOURS AT THE GERMAN NATIONAL SOCIALIST PARTY DAY AT NUREMBERG, 1933, CARRIED BY MEMBERS OF THE SA.

But it was as if some of the confusion in the country was beginning to clear – at least as far as foreign policy was concerned. The more the Chamberlain government worked to placate Hitler, the more the voice of Churchill struck a chord with the nation. When Anthony Eden resigned as Foreign Secretary in February 1938 over the government's foreign policy, particularly towards Mussolini, Churchill spoke in doom-laden words: "What price shall we all pay for this… I predict that the day will come when, at some point or other, you will have to make a stand, and I pray to God, when that day comes, that we may find, through an unwise policy, that we have to make that stand alone." One leading newspaper commented that Churchill had expressed "As on many other occasions, the widespread sentiments of anxiety and perplexity in the country." But the Cabinet – Chamberlain and Halifax in particular – were set on their course.

Austria was annexed in the spring of 1938. Then at the Munich Conference in September 1938, Czechoslovakia was sacrificed. Many thought it a good deal at the time. Chamberlain returned waving the famous piece of paper with the equally famous, now infamous, words: "I believe it is peace for our time." *The Times* thought it caught the mood of the country with the grandiose words: "No conqueror returning from a victory on the battlefield, has come home adorned with nobler laurels."

But Chamberlain was clutching at straws, not paper. And it was as if the public knew it. There were thousands of volunteers for the ARP – the Air Raid Precautions service – evacuation plans were published, air raid shelters were dug or distributed, people started leaving the cities, new wills were written and there was a sudden spate of marriages. It took a year for war to come, but it was an inevitability.

DIARIES AND LETTERS

1934 – SIR OSWALD MOSLEY

Sir Oswald Mosley, leader of the British Union of Fascists, gave Fascist tendencies in Britain a boost, partly coinciding with events in Europe. Here he expounds his political ideals.

Fascism believes that it is not beyond the genius of the British people in the present age to move with order, peace and legality to the new system of action which the problems of the age demand. Without Fascism the achievement of the totalitarian and corporate state is impossible.

The machinery must not only work, it must also live, and it can only live by the inspiration of Fascism. The new creed comes to make all things new and above all this means a change of spirit. We may devise the most perfect machinery of government and of industry. All this will count for nothing without the life and spirit of organized Fascism.

Our disciplinary manhood, winning through strength and ordeal to triumph, will provide the force and the spirit that shall prevail over material things.

MARCH 1934
– WILLIAM JOYCE

William Joyce was a particularly ardent Fascist supporter, who spoke at many rallies. In 1939 he fled to Germany, where he remained, reinventing himself as the infamous Lord Haw Haw, who made frequent pro-Nazi propaganda broadcasts on British radio throughout the duration of the war. Here he speaks at a rally in Brighton.

We know that England is crying for a leader, and that leader has emerged in the person of the greatest Englishman I have ever known, Sir Oswald Mosley...When the history of Europe comes to be written I can assure you that his name will not be second to either Mussolini or Hitler.

JUNE 1934 – RITCHIE CALDER

Richie Calder witnessed one of the popular BUF rallies in Olympia in June 1934.

I attended Olympia in a purely private capacity. I wanted to find out what Mosley had to offer. I was in the stalls in the middle of the hall. I testify that I heard no interrupters (with the exception of the man in the roof who was shouting down on top of us). But I saw plenty of interruptions. Indeed the organizers were at great pains to ensure that we should see them.

A woman who intervened in a scuffle in the body of the hall was man-handled first of all by male Blackshirts and then flung to the "tender mercies" of the female Blackshirts. There was tearing and clawing, with the woman screaming. She was stripped naked to the waist; her clothes had apparently been torn from her. As she was carried moaning past the Blue Stalls, a woman behind me rose indignantly and shouted, "Disgraceful". A Blackshirt steward leaned over towards her and said menacingly, "It will be better for you if you sit down." All this was carried out to the accompaniment of the rah-rah college yell, under a cheer-leader of, "We want Mosley – MOSLEY."

Well they can have him, I am sure no one else wants him.

SEPTEMBER 1938 – MISS MOYRA CHARLTON

Moyra Charlton was born on December 26, 1917. At the outbreak of war, she was living at home in Essex. She worked as a driver for the FANYs, and for her father who was the commander of the local Home Guard, before joining the WRNS. Miss Charlton expresses her feelings of tension as war seems inevitable, and her doubts about Chamberlain's agreement with Hitler.

SEPTEMBER 12, 1938

When we got in, Hitler's speech was in progress and the Cowells listening in. By missing some supper I managed to hear most of it, though I only understood a word here and there. The Fuehrer was theatrical and arresting, making the most of an emotional delivery.

From what I could gather in fragments from the Cowells, he means no surrender. Sooner or later he will have Czechoslovakia; his armament and defences will be ready before the autumn is out. In each pause, a crowd of thousands cheered and roared and howled. Hearing Hitler's very words and those frenzied howls brought home without doubt the terrible significance of it. Hitler means war. His people are as mad as he is, drunk with their brutal lust for gain. How can one man plunge Europe into war? Thousands, millions of young lives to be spilt – and this only twenty years after last time? It can't be, God can't let it happen. But to hear those cheers made me awfully afraid. At the end they sang "Deutschland über Alles" with swelling grandeur and poor Mrs Cowell ran out in tears. What must it be like for her, with relatives and all her friends in Germany?

ADOLF HITLER, IN THE "BROWN SHIRT" UNIFORM OF PARTY LEADER, MEETS AN ADORING SUPPORTER.

SEPTEMBER 21, 1938

The news worse than ever. The tide is turning against Chamberlain and I must say it does seem a short-sighted policy to give in to Germany over Czechoslovakia. It will not be the end but the beginning of demands, and war is bound to come sooner or later unless something phenomenal happens... This over-hanging shadow is the worst part, and Hitler may be trying out one enormous bluff. Who knows? Perhaps the end of the world is coming with Christ in His Glory – we are all in a sufficient chaos to justify the prophecy. Who knows?

SEPTEMBER 30, 1938

The new agreement seems to have given way to nearly all Hitler's demands. We heard that we were to continue issuing gas masks, so spent the afternoon at the hall. We fitted all the schoolchildren which was rather a job as we had our full issue of masks but not half enough small ones, so we had to "make do" with the mediums. By strapping them right on top of the head one can make them air-tight, if not very secure. The children en masse were much better behaved than those who came with their parents...

London went mad welcoming Chamberlain home. His devoted sincerity and tact speak for themselves, but has he done really the best thing? God knows, one moment we are preparing to annihilate Hitler, the next we are binding ourselves to a peace treaty with him behind France's back – a treaty which Chamberlain will respect and Hitler will not... What a week this has been. The speed of international politics leaves one bewildered.

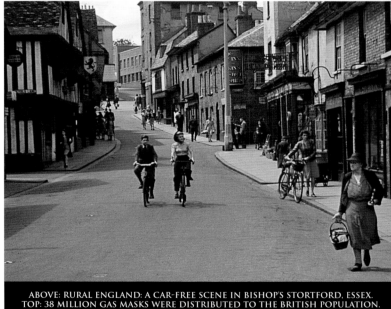

ABOVE: RURAL ENGLAND: A CAR-FREE SCENE IN BISHOP'S STORTFORD, ESSEX.
TOP: 38 MILLION GAS MASKS WERE DISTRIBUTED TO THE BRITISH POPULATION.

1940: MEMBERS OF THE WAAF POSITION BARRAGE BALLOONS. EVEN THE LITTLEWOOD'S POOLS FACTORY IN LIVERPOOL
WAS TURNED OVER TO BARRAGE BALLOON MANUFACTURE

CHAPTER II

THE PHONEY WAR

A calamitous sequence of events made war inevitable by August 1939. The growing fears of the British people were rapidly realized. On August 22, the British government announced that it would stand by its pledge to defend Poland, the latest nation to be threatened by Hitler. But the Nazi-Soviet pact was signed the next day and on August 24, Parliament was called from recess to pass the Emergency Powers Act. Military reservists were called up, the ARP told to stand by, and, on September 1, evacuations began.

However, this time, with memories of the shattered lives that followed the excitement of 1914, the mood was sombre. There was simply grim determination to "get it over with". There was also fear – fear of the new threat from the air. The population had been well enough briefed about the perils of aerial bombardment and gas attacks. Gas masks had been distributed in their millions and such was their grotesque look and smell that they all too readily suggested the horrors that awaited a vulnerable civilian population.

There was much posturing in the West, as Hitler's panzers demolished Poland, aided and abetted on the Soviet flank by Stalin's Red Army. The British Expeditionary Force sailed for France, to "dig in", just as they had in the Great War, and wait.

Back home in Britain, it seemed as if everyone was on the move. Over three and a half million people moved between June and September 1939. Civil servants were moved from London, and national treasures were hidden in caves, vaults and mine-workings. Both the authorities and the public thought it vital to get women and children out of the cities. The country was divided into "evacuation", "neutral", and "reception" areas. House-to-house surveys suggested that there were places for nearly five million people in the various "reception" areas. So it began.

On the whole it was chaotic. Some areas got far more evacuees than they had expected, some got far fewer. Some groups managed to stay together, but many were scattered over large areas. Some communities that had expected busloads of children, got instead large numbers of women and babies.

Little provision had been made in the reception areas for the long-term needs of the visitors. There were nearly a million children to educate in areas with small schools, spread across great distances. There were half a million mothers and children under school age and over 10,000 expectant mothers. Maternity facilities, midwifery care and social service provision had hardly been thought about.

Worse still was the often random billeting procedures. Some well-organized areas, with conscientious billeting officers, had logical ways of matching visitors with hosts. In other areas it was random. In some others, hosts got to pick and choose whom they would get. Of course, this meant that those with initiative and influence got to choose the pick of the crop and those without either, had to collect the residue. The inevitable resentment this caused was widespread.

But out of the chaos, British phlegm triumphed. Millions were moved, compulsion wasn't used and the people got by. But it was a shock. Rural Britain met urban Britain, middle-class Britain met working-class Britain, as never before. Large country houses were new homes for children brought up in the squalor of city tenements. Children used to hot water from the tap in the comfort of their well-off London suburb had to fetch freezing water from the well in a dingy farm worker's cottage, deep in the middle of a distant shire. But war didn't hurl itself from the skies, nor assault the British beaches. It became a "bore war" and, later a "phoney war".

While little happened in the war itself, the state of the evacuees became a national pre-occupation. Lack of toilet training, bed-wetting, vermin, head lice and scabies became the afflictions of the nation. They had all been present before, but confined to the squalid parts of the towns and cities. They had been out of sight, out of mind, but now they were dispersed all over Britain. A nation viewed itself for the first time. It didn't like what it saw.

Many evacuees drifted back. Hosts were glad to be rid of unsavoury visitors. Perfectly clean and polite visitors were glad to leave hosts whose attitudes seemed at best patronizing, at worst downright hostile. In some homes, visitors were treated like skivvies, or inmates in a detention centre. By the beginning of 1940, almost 700,000 (40% of children and 90% of mothers and children under five) had gone home.

Of course, in many instances evacuation was a success, for both the hosts and the visitors. As the war progressed and as air attacks on the cities began, evacuation planning and administration improved.

Britain took on a very unusual appearance during the Phoney War. Barrage balloons floated above the cities like fat, silver cigars. People carried gas masks, as they were required to, and sniffed the air for strange odours. Highly inflammable supplies of scotch were shipped to America for safekeeping. For a while, cinemas, theatres and sporting arenas were closed to prevent mass casualties from air attacks. Sandbags protected everything, and statues of the great and good were boarded up to save them from blast damage. Every source of light was blacked out to cloak the cities in darkness, against the prying eyes of the bomb-aimers, and every window taped up to forestall the impact of bomb blasts.

There was a strange darkness at night, not

A WOMAN WAR-WORKER BEING INSTRUCTED ON THE USE OF MACHINERY AT A FACTORY PRODUCING STEN GUNS, 1943.

A BABY SHOW, JULY 1944: A BALANCED DIET THROUGH RATIONING LED TO THE CREATION OF WHAT HAS BEEN DUBBED THE "HEALTHIEST GENERATION", GROWING UP IN THE FOUNDLING WELFARE STATE ALSO PLAYED A PART.

seen for several generations. It harked back to the days before electricity. Star-gazers, romantics and traditionalists loved it. Those with more pragmatic needs were infuriated at being unable to see their way. Lamp-posts and kerbstones became major obstacles, black-out wardens, as they soon became known, rapidly became disliked for being over-fussy, or even "little Hitlers". There was an alarming increase in motor vehicle accidents in September 1939. A Gallup poll published at the beginning of January 1940 showed that one in five people claimed to have sustained some kind of injury (mainly minor) as a result of the black-out. Eventually, the restrictions were a little less severe. Small torches were allowed, if they were dimmed with paper, restricted-beam headlamps were permitted for cars, and dimmed lights were possible for shops and restaurants.

The radio was a great comfort during the long nights of black-out. "It's That Man Again" had its first wartime airing on September 19. "ITMA" starred Tommy Handley and a team of comedians and mimics. Their irreverent humour, at the expense of officialdom, became hugely popular. "The Office of Twerps" in "The Ministry of Aggravation" struck just the right chord with an audience constantly encouraged, cajoled and harangued by official directives to promote

JIMMY O'SHEA AS "MRS MULLIGAN" IN THE BBC RADIO PROGRAMME "IRISH HALF-HOUR", 1943.

the war effort. Mrs Mopp became a legend, as did her opening line, followed by a rich vein of innuendos, "Can I do you now, sir?"

The well-known novelist, J.B. Priestley also became a radio institution. He seemed to speak for the ordinary man. His soft, northern tone contrasted with that of the other great orator of wartime, Winston Churchill. Priestley's was more a voice of the people and it had a radical edge too. So much so, that many Conservative politicians thought his words were far too "political" for the BBC to be broadcasting. However, both because of his pointed remarks, and in spite of them, he was hugely popular.

While Churchill spoke of the spirit of the people and their higher ideals, Priestley spoke about their basic needs and their gut instincts. In June 1940, he made a famous broadcast about the "little ships" which helped get the stranded troops off the beaches of Dunkirk, especially the Channel steamers:

A COVENANTER TANK MANOEUVRES ACROSS A FIELD ON EXERCISES IN 1940.

"We have called them 'the shilling sicks'. We watched them load and unload their crowds of holiday passengers – the gents full of high spirits and bottle beer, the ladies eating pork pies, the children sticky with peppermint rock." He went on to talk about the sinking of the Gracie Fields of the Isle of Wight ferry service: "… this little steamer, like all her brave and battered sisters, is immortal. She'll go sailing proudly down the years in the epic of Dunkirk. And our great grandchildren, when they learn how we began this war by snatching glory out of defeat, and then swept on to victory, may also learn how the little holiday steamers made an excursion to hell and came back glorious."

Another institution of the airwaves had a much more ominous ring to it. William Joyce had been a Fascist associate of Oswald Mosley. His propaganda broadcasts from Germany had an audience of six million in the autumn of 1939. Called "Lord Haw Haw" – a nickname originally given to the upper-class voice of Norman Baillie Stewart, one of Joyce's fellow broadcasters – he was variously listened to for comic value and out of curiosity. But, equally, he was often taken seriously and became the source of rumour and scaremongering. His audience and propaganda value declined as the war wore on and he increasingly became a figure of ridicule. Even so, he paid for his troubled presence in British wartime morale with his life. He was executed in 1946 as a traitor.

DIARIES AND LETTERS

FRIDAY APRIL 21, 1939 – MISS HELENA MOTT
Miss Mott was a single woman living in Teddington with her sister. She was 67 in 1939. She is hugely anti-Chamberlain and wary of just about all politicians. Here, she describes her feelings regarding events leading up to war.

These days, dull, mostly, have a waiting, apprehensive quality (at least for me). Waiting for anything has an unsettling affect on one – but waiting to know if a maniac is deciding to plunge a world into war strike fundamentally at every action, useful or pleasurable, and takes even the beauty out of the delicious spring – which has been more lovely than any I remember. There is the uncomfortable feeling, going by certain straws, that Chamberlain means to give us away again. No one desires peace more than I do, but it is clear to all who may read that Hitler must not be given way to. He is an evil rotten influence on mankind and should be stood up to at every turn or the world may have to suffer such a return to stone age that no nation will escape the misery and the cruelty of his regime and ideology. There's far too great a tendency – owing to Hitler's reiteration – to blame the Versailles Treaty. It may hold many a mistake that time has shown, but was evidently not severe enough, if Hitler can be tolerated.

AUGUST 22, 1939 – CATHERINE M. PHIPPS
Kate Phipps, a capable, versatile and well-educated woman, worked as a nurse. She was widely travelled and had lived in Canada just before the war. Here, she writes a letter to her friend Mrs Little of Athabasca, Canada.

Quite frankly, many of us would feel relieved if we did get this war (in spite of gas masks and possible incendiary bombs) because this crisis business hanging over us for so long is very nerve wracking. One doesn't know what Hitler will do next, and I ask myself why should we all live at the beck and call of these dictators! I haven't slept at all well the last few weeks, and some people are getting a bit jittery, and expecting to be annihilated at any moment by bombers that cross the coast unannounced! One hopes if that happens that

NEVILLE CHAMBERLAIN DRIVES TO MEET HITLER IN MUNICH, 1938.

one will cop a nice clean hit, and not linger on badly injured or having to clear up the mess with inadequate help. Selfish no doubt, but that's the way some of us feel! Don't get too shocked.

Is the world going crazy? One hears that Hitler has just signed a pact with Russia. After getting Spain and Italy, and I believe Japan, to sign an anti comintern pact, he now says that Germany and Russia have identical interests and culture. I sincerely hope NOT! What's he up to?

I don't altogether trust Mr Chamberlain and suppose he had to do all that flying to Munich last year…but one felt so ashamed about Czechoslovakia. I made friends with a Czech woman doc at the Mat Hospital, she told me a lot…she is now a refugee, but isn't allowed to function as a doc…only as a midwife…too bad isn't it.

You asked about Lord Halifax…he is very high church, more Rome than the pope they say, and not well I gather so not really one in whom the nation should put trust. They say "rien comprendre c'est tout pardoner" in his connection, meaning he's not too bright. I wouldn't know. It is probably only a bright quip. I picked it up from a naval officer! Yes, I'm meeting all sorts of folk over here, I don't feel you will see me for a long long time.

Meanwhile bye for now etc etc…

SEPTEMBER 1939 – CATHERINE M. PHIPPS
Kate was billeted to a first aid post in late 1939.

Dear Friends,
Excitement at last I'm in the war! For so long we have been expecting and preparing for this, and now it's here one can't help feeling a bit relieved! I'm at the first aid post in London. I suppose I shouldn't say where! Anyway pretty old fashioned "square" with trenches in the process of being dug where the lawn used to be. In front of the hospital are posted men of the Auxiliary Fire Brigade [sic] with an engine painted grey. They have a sandbagged shelter with gas proof airlock, but they prefer sitting outside as the weather is very good just now.

Protective clothing has arrived at the Post and gas lectures started. I am unfortunately exempt owing to have taken it last year. However we all to practise decontaminating the bathroom! The clothing consists of yellow oilskin trousers, three quarter length coats ditto, wellington boots, hoodlike headgear, gloves and masks. Ye gods what all this must be costing the government! They told us at the Aldershot camp that one can't work more than half an hour in this rig out owing to the heat. We have been advised to buy pots of bleach paste for personal use and to carry them always in our GM cases. There is already a shortage.

Great arguments as to where wounded gas casualties are to be treated, does one treat wounds first or gas? At what point are they removed from contaminated stretchers? Are contaminated dead to be decontaminated or kept separate from the "clean corpses"? If it wasn't so serious it would be ludicrous… And now we have instructions to carry our gas masks to meals!

Miss J Twitters, Mrs SD Flaps and the outsiders

who are taking the course snigger. I and a couple of others armed with Chemical Warfare certificates feel superior, remembering our Army Instructor made us all shout in chorus in answer to his question "What do you do first on receiving the first warning 'gas attack'?" … "ATTEND TO THE WANTS OF NATURE." I also remember coming out of those very down to earth horrifying lectures and seeing a pool of oil in the road and giving it a wide berth in case it was mustard gas! How hallucinated can one get over all this?

SEPTEMBER 1, 1939 – MRS M. DINEEN

Mrs Dineen, aged about 35, was evacuated from her home in Streatham, London, with her two children, first to Eastbourne and then to South Wales. Her husband stayed at home and worked as an ARP warden. Here, Mrs Dineen describes her evacuation journey.

The great evacuation of schoolchildren from London began for us at 7.30am on Sept. 1st 1939. We all arrived at school fully equipped with clothing, gas mask and food for the great unknown journey.

Children were very excited, the older ones perhaps a little scared, helpers and teachers worried and mothers with sad eyes but brave smiles.

Everyone was most anxious to be on our way and we arrived at the station in a very short time. All was very quiet here, no people on the platform, only lines of children all looking forward to a journey in a train. At last we heard the whistle and with shouts and cheers everyone was aboard and we were off. From the windows we watched London fade away and saw the green fields of Surrey and later on the hills of Sussex come into view.

We realized we must be going to the sea as the stations flashed by, and presently we heard the cry of "All change Eastbourne". It is now 11. We marched from the station in our lines of five, with crowds looking on. We might have been film stars arriving, the attention we received. After a rest the children were examined by a doctor and we again marched off to receive our rations for the 1st 24 hours. These were very good, 2 tins of Corned Beef, 1 tin Ideal Milk, 1 tin Nestles Milk, 1lb Biscuits & 4d Bar Milk Chocolate.

Everyone was most kind and made us all feel welcome. Then began our search for our temporary home.

We were taken by billeting officers to various houses and in a very short time we were all found accommodation, some were luckier than others but that is always so.

SEPTEMBER 3, 1939 – MRS GWLADYS COX

Gwladys Cox was born in Jamaica in 1885. She moved to London with her husband in the 1920s. They had no children. Here, Mrs Cox feels strongly patriotic as war is declared.

On returning home, we turned on the wireless and heard there was to be "an important announcement" by the Prime Minister at 11.15 a.m. So with bated breath – the whole world was on tiptoe of expectancy this morning – we settled ourselves in the sitting room and listened to Mr Chamberlain's broadcast.

He announced that, as there had been no reply by 11 a.m. to our ultimatum, we, as a nation, were at war with Germany.

I shall never forget the thrill of his closing words:– "Now, may God bless you all. May He defend the right. It is the evil things we shall be fighting against – brute force, bad faith, injustice, oppression and persecution. And, against them, I am certain that the right will prevail."

Mr Chamberlain's speech was followed by the playing of "God Save the King", for which I rose and remained standing until it was finished.

SEPTEMBER 10, 1939 – MRS GWLADYS COX

As the blackout is put into effect in London, Mrs Gwladys Cox notes that it is causing accidents.

There is, now, no street lighting whatever at night, except very diminished traffic lights; the result is a complete black-out. It is the duty of the A.R.P. wardens to patrol the streets and warn householders when they see any light whatsoever visible through their curtains. The staircase in our block is in complete darkness at night, no easy matter to stumble up and down, groping for bannisters. All motor headlights are very severely restricted, likewise interior lighting of buses, so accidents are frequent. Jane tells me that St Mary's, Paddington, vacuated for war casualties, is now busy with black-out casualties. The darkness outside is intense, and to walk along the street and cross the road at night is a real adventure. In consequence, practically all shops are closing at, or before dusk, and the streets of West Hampstead are deserted by sunset.

ERNEST BRADFIELD

Ernest Bradfield from East Ham, London, was 13 when he was evacuated to Cornwall with his younger brother, Stuart. His letters home, which are undated, show that life was not always happy for evacuees.

Dear Mum and Dad… Yes Stu' and I have changed billets… This time she didn't get rid of us, we got rid of her. It was like this, we were comfortable and the place was clean, but she used to do underhand things. For instance take my letters and read them when I wasn't there and forage about generally. Also she wanted the £..s..d but not the trouble. Always nagging Stu' when I was not within earshot. Something like this – Stuart tears blazer. "Oh, bout time you could sew this yourself." Then when giving him a good wash, "about time you could wash yourself. Terry does." And the last was that the food wasn't so hot. Terry and Norman were getting twice as much as us. I had made arrangements beforehand about our billets. Then when she said that we had better find another home, everyone was on her like a ton of bricks. And that was that.

Dear Mum and Dad, Now that you have upset me and broken your promises I suppose you are satisfied. Well if it is the last earthly thing I do I am coming home Christmas. You made promise after promise about that. You're OK. I don't see why I shouldn't be. What a birthday I'll have now. I'll be more use in London that down here. All I'm being here is a blinking nuisance to Cornwall and the government. You think the Blitz will frighten me. If it's lucky.

You think we are settled don't you? As you

know, Stuart has been moved or "got rid of" no less than five times, and it is my painful duty to announce that he may be moved again in the near future... Sometimes I feel like cutting my throat. Thank goodness I'm nearly 14 now. I'll be glad when I'm 15 so that this will be just history.

SEPTEMBER 23, 1939
– MISS FLORENCE SPEED

Florence Speed has a friend who lives in Sussex and who frequently furnishes her with details of life in the country, including problems with the billeting of evacuees.

At Penshurst Place they have 50 evacuees,

mothers and children. Some of them are awful _ dirty and really lousy. Sally's mother has taken a Science Master and his wife, fearing worse. The Dulwich and Westminster boys have of course been snapped up.

The billeting officer had a ghastly job finding a home for a mother of 5 with another baby on the way who refused to be parted from any of them.

In one house there are 3 mothers with their children. They all have to cook at different times! Not much hope for the householders!

One boy returned to his billet with a cabbage and some apples. "Cor, you don't have to buy them here," he said, "They grow wild." A woman stopped at Tonbridge and said,

"Where's the bloody street with the bloody draper's shop?" "There's a policeman down the road, ask him," was the curt retort.

"There's not an apple left in Leigh, so Sally says – the children have just helped themselves.

SEPTEMBER 28, 1939 – MISS JOAN STRANGE
Joan Strange was a single woman in her thirties living with her mother in Worthing. A committed Christian and professional masseuse, she was very concerned with the international situation and became involved with aiding refugees from occupied Europe.

I had my hair repermed as it was so bad. Warsaw falls or "dropped" as Fritz Krauz reported it! Terrible ordeal of the inhabitants. England to support the Save the Children fund next Sunday at all churches. *The Daily Telegraph* reported that the pilot of one of our "leaflet" planes reported back at headquarters two hours before he was due. His astonished CO asked for an explanation. "Well Sir," the young officer replied, "I flew over enemy territory as instructed and tipped out the parcels over the side." "Do you mean you threw them out still wrapped up in bundles?" said the CO in an anxious voice. "Yes Sir." "Good God, man, you might have killed somebody!" Then there was the pilot who turned up two hours too late! Explanation this time was that he'd been as quick as possible, pushing them under people's doors.

OCTOBER 1939 –
SIGNALMAN JACK DALE
Jack Dale was in service with the Royal Corps of Signals when he arrived with the BEF in France in September 1939. He writes to his parents in Coventry.

OCTOBER 3, 1939
Dear Mother and Dad
I have just moved again and am writing to say I am still well and happy… We are now staying at a big farm and are billets are inside a building just above the house of the farmer… We have travelled a long time way since we left England and I am surprised at the amount of fruit trees we passed. There are apples, pears, peaches and grapes in the hundred. The churches over here are very pretty, mostly Roman Catholic and at lonely parts of the roads there are crucifixes making the place look very sacred. I have got a small booklet of French and English and am learning quite a nice little bit in my spare time, you would be surprised how hard to it is to pick it up and talk so as to make yourself understood, but it grand fun. When we are travelling & come to a big town, the people seem very glad to see us, they wave and cheer and if we stop they bring out biscuits and dainties for us to eat. The only shortage here is fags, English I mean, there are French cigarettes of course but they do not smoke the same as an English one. I am at present smoking my pipe as this does not go down too bad with French tobacco. For the present Bonne Nuit (Good night). Your loving son Jack.

OCTOBER 5, 1939
Dear Mother & Dad
Well how are you keeping at home, keeping

fit I hope, have you had any raids at Coventry yet? Are we stopping all the enemy ok this end? Well I haven't met dat guy Hitler yet, he must be hiding…but he will have to come out for fresh air someday and then we will give him de woiks and dat will be dat merci boco…Well today we had a grand dinner, roast beef, roast potatoes, and a small mash, consisting of turnips and carrots and oh boy wasn't it grand. I have had good meals since I've been here consisting of stews mostly and today was a very good treat… Well there is still no news to tell so for now cheerio. Lots of love your loving son John.

OCTOBER 7, 1939
Dear Mother and Dad

Just a small note to say I am still well and happy. The weather here is still holding out good, & we still continue to make this army life pleasant. You can have a grand night out here for about 1/6 d. Last night I went to a café and had steak and chips which cost only 5.50 francs and Benedictine 1 franc per glass. I have not received your parcel yet so I think by now it has been lost…not much news to tell you at present, only I am still somewhere in France. Well hoping you are all well and happy at home. Your loving son, Jack.

OCTOBER 16, 1939
– MISS JOAN STRANGE

In the early days of war, Joan Strange, notes the changes in everyday life.

A lovely day. Shopped and coffee'd in the morning. Cheltenham very full of "vacks" and the shops full of all the usual ARP goods. One gets sick of looking at black stuff, gas mask cases, identity card cases, buckets and shovels (for removing incendiary bombs), low powered bulbs, black shades, etc. The buses' windows are all blued over and give one a sick feeling whilst travelling. Heard at four o'clock the wireless message that German bombers had attacked the Firth of Forth but missed the Forth bridge. Four German planes were brought down. The first air-raid on Britain.

NOVEMBER 28, 1940 – MISS JOAN STRANGE

Miss Strange is indignant at hearing the propaganda programmes aired by Lord Haw Haw [alias William Joyce] following the end of the Phoney War.

Just before I came to bed Lord Haw Haw forced his way in to the English programme – everything was false. According to him we'd lost 300 planes in Greece to the Italian fifty, the Albanians resent the Greeks coming through their country, Great Britain is in dire straits for fresh fruit, milk and eggs! The d*** swine! I really delight in swearing at this traitor and his lies. There is a lot of sabotage going on in Norway and in Paris hundreds of students have been imprisoned by the Germans. The Germans tried to alienate the Parisians from Britain recently by showing the "cruelty of the RAF". When the pictures showing damage to Germany appeared the audience got up and cheered and cheered! In England there is a growing feeling of confidence spreading. Food is plentiful on the whole – certainly eggs are scarce (Mollie gave us seventeen on Sunday which was lovely) but no one need go hungry. Blackout lasts from 5.30 to 8.20 am now owing to daylight saving still being in force – it's to enable Londoners to get home before the blitz starts.

JANUARY 31, 1940
– MRS OLIVE COUZENS

Olive Couzens, née Lewis, from Southgate, London N11, trained as a teacher during the war. She is writing to her fiancé, Leslie, who is a stretcher bearer with the London Rifle Brigade and is posted to various places around England. Here, Olive replies to a letter from Leslie expressing his depression at being in the forces.

MEMBERS OF THE ROYAL OBSERVER CORPS ON DUTY ON THE SOUTH COAST, 1940.

Sweetheart,

I am so distressed at your heartbreaking letter. Its tone of mental anguish, of hopelessness frightens me. Frightens me when I think of the harm it can do to you if it conquers your own willpower. In this war we are fighting not only against a threat of terrorism but, while it lasts, that mental stagnation which perforce follows. It is of little comfort for me to say that others are equally sick, but it is true, and even you yourself have said it. I feel every pain you feel, ache for your loss of liberty, despair with the knowledge of a rotting mind and the very small help I can give is to assure you that I feel for you in every way and of every minute; your thoughts and feelings are here inside me as if they were my own.

But my dearest I beg of you have courage.

I hate to see someone I love being crushed by a despairing attitude.

As a prayer from me which I hope will be granted – I am longing for your transfer; – and may it be soon.

MAY 16, 1940

By May 1940, Olive Couzens is showing determination and a will to win.

I'm very puzzled with the International situation at the moment. I can't see why if Germany can bomb open towns, why our planes can't pop over Berlin & give them a little of their own medicine. You know I fancy if our pilots gave Berlin such hell continuously as the Germans gave Rotterdam they would be in the same nervous condition as the Dutch were and they would willingly give in – Only theoretical I admit but if they had a dose of real war (not experienced even in the Great War) they would not be so ready to revere militarism.

Perhaps London fears reprisals, but then isn't it fear & hesitancy that has brought us to this?

Lots & lots & lots of love sweetheart

JUNE 6, 1940 – MISS I.H. GRANGER

Miss Granger, from London, was a teacher in her early thirties when war broke out. She hated her job and became an investigator for the Unemployment Assistance Board. She expresses her feelings about the war in a series of letters to a friend in Canada. Here she expresses her uncertainty about the future following the Phoney War.

It has been for weeks now the most glorious summer I can remember: each day is full of east wind which makes a perfectly blue sky whose vividness is enhanced by swaying silver barrage balloons: they come down periodically & look like khaki pigs, but from the garden they are like silver fish & only serve to beautify the sky. Except for the almost ceaseless thunder of guns, it is impossible, in the garden, to believe in the war – then cynically I

AN RAF PILOT, 1940.

remind myself that such loveliness as is being lavished on me now must surely be the prelude to annihilation.

However, in London now it is fruitless to speculate for more than an hour or two ahead, so all one's hours are valuable gay things & in a personal way I can find myself curiously happy. I never remember such long days in sunshine, quite unsultry and full of flowers, in London before – I wonder if it is the prelude to the end, a special treat for the condemned man before the gallows, or is it a presage & a consolation. The exaggeration of beauty of this spring has seemed sometimes to mock & to be intolerable in its serenity and confidence.

AUGUST 2, 1940 – MISS I.H. GRANGER
Miss Granger is angered by the suffering and injustice she sees.

Perhaps the most cruel stories are those of the men between 45–55 whose firms closed down last September: French polishers, advertising supervisors, compositors, people whose trades of a life time have been hit by various rationing schemes. They are too old for the army, too young for a pension & inaction: they are bitter, degraded at the sight of their wives who "do a bit of cleaning" to keep the home together, they resent accepting help from their seventeen or nineteen year old children who work as machinists or counter hands at 16/- – 25/- a week. It's a cruel irony to burden these children with the keep of a physically fit father, whose means of livelihood has been destroyed by our system,

is a cause of untold family bitterness. It all makes me savagely angry.

SPRING 1941 – SYBIL AND LEILA ROTHSTEIN
The Rothstein were two Jewish sisters who were evacuated to Nottinghamshire from Worthing in early 1941. Sybil was 11 and Leila, 6. Here are Sybil's and Leila's first letters to their parents on reaching their billet.

Dear Mummy + Daddy

We had a very long journey which started at nine and ended at five-o-clock. During our journey we saw lots of barrage balloons. Leila was thrilled with the baby lambs we saw. When we arrived at Newark we stayed the night at Newark Technical Colledge where everybody was very kind to us. We slept on mattresses with two or three thick blankets over us. We also slept in our jerseys. We all had some food left over from the journey so we had a midnight feast when the staff had gone. P.T.O. [page 2] We set off for Ollerton at eleven twenty five. Leila + I cried a little when we arrived at our billets but I think we'll be all right. I want ever so much to come home although Mrs Farrow is nice. I hope you are keeping all right. Is grandad better? Mrs Farrow is going to write to-night.

Your loving daughter,

Sybil XXXXXXXXXXXXXXXXXXXXX

MARCH 24, 1941

Dear Mummy + Daddy

How are you getting on. My doll has not arrived yet, I heard about my byce and I would like you to send it for me. I have got a husband and his name is Kenneth Farrow, P.T.O. [page 2] when I come home do you think There will be any room for my husband, I was thinking that he could work at Jordan and Cook, I would take him the first day. If he doesent come he will come on my birthday with the rest of the family. We went to Mansfeild and Forest town with Mr Farrow on Satureday. Please send me a scarf because it is verry cold. Pamala Portuies has moved because she was unhappy. My birthday is the same day as my husband's brother's birthday, his name is Ronny. When I am reddy to marry kenneth he'll be 27 and I will be twenty. Kenneth is a nice looking boy.

    Love to all, Leila

24.4.41

Dear Mummy + Daddy,

    I hope you are keeping well. I am getting used to it now. Most people seem to think that we're only staying here until the invasion scare is over, not till the end of the war. Will you please send us scarves? It is cold up here. The case had not arrived when I wrote this letter but perhaps by the time you will have received it, it will have arrived. We've had a lot of bother about Leila's schooling. This morning I sat with her in her classroom but I thought if I sat with her always she'd never get used to it, so I took her to school this afternoon and told her teacher what I thought. She agreed with me and so I went to my own lesson. Leila cried then, but I think she'll get used to it in time. One morning Leila was homesick and I didn't know how to comfort her. (I was in bed) I asked her what would happen if all the soldiers cried

and we never won the war.

    I am sure you will enjoy Leila's very amusing letter. What do you think about her + Kenneth? Mrs Farrow thinks it will be all right to send Leila's bike because Leila wants it. Mr + Mrs Farrow are very, very kind to us. I like Ronny & Kenneth very much, and they like us.

    Much love, Sybil.
    328 Walesby Lane
    New Ollerton

TUESDAY

Disturbed by Leila's behaviour, Mrs Farrow writes to Leila's parents.

    328 Walesby Lane
    New Ollerton

Dear Mr & Mrs Rothstein

    Just a few lines in answer to yours we received Monday morning, I was sorry Sybil had to write and tell you that they was not warm enough in bed but I don't know how many clothes they do want as they sleep, between flannelette blankets they have 3 wool blankets to cover them a wilt and a thick eiderdown and then the fire is under the bedroom all day, Sybil is still a good girl but this last fortnight Leila has been awfull if I speak to her she turns her nose up at me and will not answer me in fact she ignores me altogether and it is making me feel miserable as I am sure I have been ever so good to her but I have told her tonight she does ought to try and be a good girl as I am saying Sybil is like an angel not a bit of trouble and we treat them just as if they were our own.

Miss Kent came to see us Monday night and she thought they was two lucky girls to have got such a good home but she said she was going to write you to let you know they was alright as some of her childrens parents had been over and it had unsettled them again, but if you care to come any time and you can put up with the best of what we can give you as you will understand what it is like we have 3 bedrooms and each on is a double bed in so my husband says we can make do just for a weekend with one or two extra anything to [page 3] oblige. Well Mrs Rothstein I am sorry I have had to write and tell you this about Leila but we thought if you just wrote to her it would made a difference as I don't like her to be like that and I will write again next week and let you know how we are going on so I shall have to close this time give our kind regards to Mr Rothstein.

I remain

Mr & Mrs Farrow and boys

PS Leila has told me she is going to try and be a good girl I don't think she likes it because I have told you. Miss Kent thought Leila did look well she could not help but look at her.

SATURDAY AT SCHOOL.

22.4.41

Dear Mummy + Daddy

How are you getting on. If you would like to no I am getting a hole in my green dress. Aunty Vi says its Because I'm getting to fat, when Miss Kent came she said I looked a lot Better. Aunty Vi says I've been a good girl last week P.T.O. [page 2] I'm sorry that I've beend naughty girl. I am pleased to know that you are knitting me a jumper to go with my scotch kilt. Because I have only my red jumper There is nothink realy nice to wear for school. I like the tips on the shoes very [page 3] much. I had two weeks holaday for easter. The first class I was in was Miss Doleys, class 2 I have onley been in her class 5 weeks and I went up yester day into a class called Miss Kelt, she is not very nice. I like Miss Doley. I go out to play nearly evry day. It is Aunty Vi's P.T.O... Well bye bye lots of love to evrybod. Mrs and Mr Farrow and Ken and Ron send there love. Love from your loving daughter Leila.

THROUGHOUT THE SUMMER OF 1939 BRITAIN'S NEWSPAPERS REPORTED EVERY TWIST AND TURN OF EVENTS LEADING UP TO THE OUTBREAK OF WAR.

SOLDIERS AT AN ARMY PHYSICAL TRAINING SCHOOL, c. 1940: UNEMPLOYMENT AND POOR NUTRITION IN THE 1930S MADE IT NECESSARY TO IMPROVE PHYSICAL FITNESS AS WELL AS TEACH MILITARY SKILLS TO THIS NEW ARMY.

CHAPTER III

WAR IN THE WEST

Neville Chamberlain had managed to survive as Prime Minister despite the debacle of Munich and the sacrifice of Czechoslovakia. But Churchill had been brought into a War Cabinet as First Lord of the Admiralty. The main parties had agreed to an electoral truce and the predominant view – shared, significantly, by the press – was that, with the country at war with Germany, it was not the time to be changing the leadership. So Chamberlain continued in office. The Labour Party continued its position of moderation. They refused to join the government, but declared themselves as a "patriotic opposition".

But Chamberlain's secure position didn't last long. With the exception of some significant naval engagements, the perception grew that Chamberlain was both failing to engage the enemy and failing to mobilize the country sufficiently to meet the inevitable challenge. The view grew that Chamberlain's ingrained political instincts not to interfere too much in the economy and to avoid a major conflagration with Germany, were unacceptable in a wartime leader.

The disaster of Britain's first major offensive of the war, in Norway in April and May 1940, provided the catalyst that led to Chamberlain's downfall. Chamberlain was no more nor less responsible for events in Norway than anybody else. In fact, if anyone were to have shouldered the blame, it should have been Churchill. But the criticisms focused more on the general state of Britain's preparedness for war than on the details of the Norwegian campaign. Chamberlain "carried the can". Churchill had wanted to land British and French forces at Narvik on the northern Norwegian coast months earlier, but couldn't get approval in the War Cabinet. When they did eventually land, it was too late and, ultimately, they had to be evacuated.

In the debate in the House of Commons which followed, the Conservative MP, Leo Amery, invoked the words of Oliver Cromwell spoken to the Long Parliament 300 years earlier in sealing the fate of the Prime Minister: "You have sat too long for any good you have been doing. Depart, I say, and let us have done with you. In the name of God, go!"

Churchill wasn't the automatic choice to succeed Chamberlain. He was still mistrusted and his enemies had long memories. Lord Halifax was the preferred choice of many. But Halifax would have had to lead from the House of Lords, and this tipped the balance in Churchill's favour. The die was cast. Britain had a leader who had always believed it was his destiny to lead his country in the hour of its greatest need. He had been proved right. He began the task immediately, in a way that perhaps no one else could have done. But even on the day he was asked to form his government, disaster struck. Germany launched

JUNE, 1940: IN A PRIVATE LETTER FROM HIS WIFE, CHURCHILL WAS CAUTIONED AGAINST HIS WORSENING MANNER TOWARDS HIS COLLEAGUES AND THE NEED FOR MORE CONSIDERATION.

its invasion in the West; the Phoney War was over and for the British the real war had begun. Britain was soon to stand alone as Luxembourg, Belgium, Holland and France were added to Norway and Denmark as German conquests.

But the more adversity struck, the more defiant Churchill sounded. Suddenly, the "maverick" became the bulwark; the "warmonger" became the only hope for peace; the "oppressor of the working-class" became the protector of freedom. Famous words flowed readily over the following months:

> *"I have nothing to offer but blood, toil, tears and sweat."*

> *"You ask, what is our policy? I will say: It is to wage war, by sea, land and air, with all our might and with all the strength that God can give us: to wage war against a monstrous tyranny, never surpassed in the dark, lamentable catalogue of human crime."*

> *"What is our aim?.... victory, victory at all costs, victory in spite of all*

terror, victory, however long and hard the road may be; for without victory there is no survival."

"...we shall defend our Island, whatever the cost may be, we shall fight on the beaches, we shall fight on the landing grounds, we shall fight in the fields and in the streets, we shall fight in the hills; we shall never surrender."

Slowly but surely, Churchill became the fulcrum, the rock upon which Britain's hopes took refuge. It was as if the people knew that he meant what he said, and as long as he said it, they believed it and stood behind him. Word spread that he really did care. He had been seen in tears when visiting bomb-damaged houses in the East End. Vernon Bartlett, an Independent MP, summed up the mood by describing the impact Churchill had on the House of Commons. "He would share with us facts and figures which seemed, on any basis of logic, to add up to inevitable and imminent disaster. But his own stubborn courage made nonsense of logic, and we would troop out of the House at the end of the debate, feeling that Britain was invincible."

The Fall of France, initiated by the German attack through the Ardennes, was prefaced when the British Expeditionary Force and tens of thousands of French comrades were trapped on the beaches of Dunkirk. The circumstances of Hitler's decision not to press on with his advance to capture the Allied forces remain something of a mystery. Perhaps he still thought Britain would join with him, in his fight against Germany's "enemies", or at least sue for peace.

In any case, the survival and removal of almost 340,000 British and French soldiers from Dunkirk became the stuff of legends. Churchill called it a "miracle of deliverance". So it was. The little ships and boats had gone and braved the Luftwaffe: Agincourt and the repulse of the Armada were invoked as victory was made out of military catastrophe. The truth of it was that the army was on its knees. Many of those who had served in France were resentful about poor leadership from their officers, morale was in a dire state and Britain was practically defenceless. But again Churchill spoke on June 18, four days after the Germans had entered Paris. His speech contained perhaps his most quoted phrase. It also named the next crisis that Britain would face.

"What General Weygand called the Battle of France is over. I expect that the Battle of Britain is about to begin... Let us therefore brace ourselves to our duties, and so bear ourselves that, if the British Empire and its Commonwealth last for a thousand years, men will still say, 'This was their finest hour.'"

Again, Britain took on a bizarre facade. Anywhere the enemy could conceivably land a plane on the south coast was blocked by some kind of hazard, many of them somewhat "Heath Robinson"

ABOVE: A BRITISH ARMY SOLDIER CRAWLS OVER AN IMPASSABLE SECTION OF LAND ON SUSPENDED ROPES.
TOP: COMMANDOS DURING BASIC TRAINING EXERCISES, IN AN UNSPECIFIED SPOT IN ENGLAND.

in design. Old cars and pieces of agricultural machinery were scattered around fields to prevent airborne landings. Similar techniques were used to block roads. Parked cars had to be immobilized by removing the rotor arm from the distributor. It was also ordered that signposts and street names be removed. They didn't reappear for almost three years in the towns, and three and a half years in the countryside. Destinations were even removed from buses, trains and trams. And, in what must have seemed like the final insult to tradition, church bells were ordered to be silent, unless rung by the police or military to warn of an airborne attack. If the invasion came, while the regular army tried to hold back the panzers, the defence of the citizenry would be entrusted to the Local Defence Volunteers. On July 23, 1940, they were renamed, The Home Guard.

FORMERLY THE LOCAL DEFENCE VOLUNTEER FORCE, IT WAS RENAMED THE HOME GUARD IN 1940.

When Anthony Eden appealed for volunteers for the LDV on May 14, the most eager were at the doors of local police stations as the broadcast finished. There were a million and a half of them by the end of June. En masse, they represented Britain at its best – and worst. There were plenty of Colonel Blimps, a caricature created by cartoonist David Low to typify the retired army officer, somewhat irascible and with strong jingoistic sentiments. There were lots of Captain Manwearings, a much later television caricature of the provincial bank manager aspiring to be a "toff" and there were creaky old men, crusty veterans, spivs and ineffectual young men. But, though it was a "Dad's Army", it was a spontaneous army; a citizen army. Owners and tenants marched together, as did management and workers.

Initially, weapons and uniforms had to be improvized. But, not unlike the Fyrd of Anglo-Saxon England, anything of a weighty or pointed

42ND ARMOURED DIVISION NEAR MALTON, YORKSHIRE IS OBSERVED BY ANTHONY EDEN, FOREIGN SECRETARY AND GENERAL SIR BERNARD PAGET, 1942.

NAIK YESHWANT GHADGE, AGED 22, WAS AWARDED THE VICTORIA CROSS POSTHUMOUSLY FOR HIS ACTIONS IN 1944 IN THE UPPER TIBER VALLEY, ITALY. HERE HIS WIFE AND SON ACCEPT IT ON HIS BEHALF.

nature was made ready to confront the enemy. Axes, hammers, billhooks, poles (fashioned to replicate pikes and halberds) and knives were typical of the armoury. Volunteers sat at home with their wives in the evening and prepared one of the most potent of all weapons of urban warfare – the Molotov Cocktail (the petrol bomb). Uniforms were equally sporadic and improvized, and included everything from trilbies and bowlers to pin-stripe suits and overalls.

The situation wasn't quite so farcical for long. Appropriate uniforms and weapons did appear, as did a logical purpose and appropriate training. Eventually they resembled a part-time regular army and looked much the same. Tens of thousands of them manned anti-aircraft guns and fulfilled many more vital military functions. How they would have performed should they ever have been tested, defending the streets and lanes of Britain, we shall never know.

As well as recruiting a citizen army, Britain also enlisted its Empire, its Commonwealth and its Dominions for support. As well as those recruits, many who had escaped from conquered Europe fled to Britain to fight another day. Many a member of the Home Guard, who thought he'd nabbed a German spy, was disconcerted to find he'd accosted a Polish airman or a Czechoslovak infantry officer. All corners of the Empire and Commonwealth supported the home

A GURKHA SOLDIER, 1945. GURKHAS HAD BEEN RECRUITED IN NEPAL SINCE THE 19TH CENTURY.

country in its hour of need. Thousands of Australians, New Zealanders, Canadians, and Indians had lost their lives by the end of the war.

Just as Britain was warmly welcoming all comers to fight for the cause, so it was turning on some who might reasonably have been described as its own. The justified internment of Nazi sympathizers took on a distinctly xenophobic feel as hostility was directed at anyone with a German-sounding name, even if they were second- or third-generation British. Italian restaurants had their windows smashed. One veteran of the First World War, who had won the Victoria Cross, was turned down for the Home Guard because of his German origins. When the systematic round-up of Germans began, it included, in a bizarre and frightening irony, many anti-Nazis who had escaped to Britain to avoid persecution in Germany. Some of these were Jewish. Harsh times demand harsh measures, but the unnecessary internment and deportation of many anti-Nazi aliens and guests was one of the most unpleasant aspects of Britain at war.

DIARIES & LETTERS

SUNDAY 12 NOVEMBER, 1939
– MRS GWLADYS COX

Gwladys Cox has sympathy for Winston Churchill's attitude towards the Germans.

A grey, dull, muggy day, but mild. This evening, we were heartened by a robust broadcast from the First Lord of the Admiralty, Mr Winston Churchill "Ten Weeks of War". It is really very jolly listening to Mr Churchill because he is not afraid to speak up and makes no bones about his contempt for the gangsters now ruling Germany. Unfortunately, all do not agree as to the suitability of his language and call it "undignified" and "war-mongering". There have been several letters to the Press from these white-livered gentry, who object to the Germans being called "Huns". If, however, they behave like Huns, I cannot see the objection.

APRIL–MAY, 1940 – C. BAGGS

C. Baggs was a member of the 1st Battalion Tyneside Scottish in France and spent April–May 1940 fighting between Abbeville and Arras. He is captured by the Germans near Arras and is taken to a transit camp.

This is some dump, thousands of POWs here all nationalities, and in open fields. The Jerry opened a gate and just like cattle we were counted in, then sat down in the grass, wondering what next move would be. Night fall and not a great coat among us, we had to lie where we were and not even a warm drink, in fact we were eating grass and clover. If you dared move during the night a shot would ring out, so if you wanted to make water etc you had to do your business where you were. Some of the village women and a Catholic father came along the road, with some bread and asked the guards if they could give it to the POW. The guards smiled, said yes, then stood back and watched the riot. Believe me, I never saw such a mob in my life, about 2,000 rushed to the fence and it was murder fighting to get a piece of bread. It was like feeding the ducks.

MAY 1940 – MRS MARY BLOOMFIELD

Mary Bloomfield was a policeman's wife from Coventry. She was 27 when war broke out. She describes the fear, particularly among women, of a German invasion.

The Germans advance through Belgium and Holland and then to France. We were all astounded by their speed. Also they were in Norway, Sweden and the Baltic Ports. Everyone suddenly woke up to their particular dangers. News had been coming in of parachutists dressed as clergymen etc. landing in Norway and we first heard the word "Quisling". Those who opposed them were gunned down, even little children. Fear and horror began to take a grip on us... Women were particularly afraid as we heard that if you were young, healthy and able to conceive you might be shipped to Germany to a "baby farm" to be mated to Germans... We all decided we ought to have a pile of hand grenades in the bedroom near the windows in case the Germans and their tanks came up our street.

MAY 6, 1940 – MISS I.H. GRANGER

Miss Granger is delighted at the resignation of Neville Chamberlain, the Prime Minister.

H.B. my dear, A short journal under the terror – a terror prefaced by the latest set of invasions this morning, but very softened by Chamberlain's resignation, announced by his own voice an hour or so ago: had the suave

WELL OVER ONE MILLION CANADIAN SERVICEMEN AND
SERVICEWOMEN ENLISTED TO SERVE THE ALLIED WAR EFFORT.

accents of the B.B.C. told me of this I should have hesitated to believe it, but I think it must be true since I heard the click of his tongue against those long front teeth of his while he announced the best news I have heard for a long time.

MAY 15–19, 1940 – SERGEANT L.D. PEXTON

Sergeant Pexton from Hull describes the German Blitzkreig in northern France.

MAY 15, 1940

"Stood to" at 3.30am. Very quiet up to 4:15am. German spotting plane came over pretty low and went back. 6.30am first taste of bombers. 68 of them all trying to create Hell upon Earth together. What a day. Just about blew us out of the ground. Got shelled all day. Getting very warm around here now don't mind the bombs as much as the planes' machine guns. They're wicked.

MAY 16, 1940

Stood to again at dawn. Quiet. Told they had come through Luxembourg with four armoured divisions but that they could only last until Sunday with petrol. MUST hold them at all costs. Still more shelling. Cambrai must be in a mess by now. Got some more bombs today.

MAY 17, 1940

Dawn again. Lovely morning. Can't believe war is anywhere near. Refugees still pouring out of Cambrai. I am only 50 yards from main Cambrai-Arras Road. Big steel bridge not far from my dugout. Heard from boy commander today that engineers will blow it up if he gets too near.

MAY 18, 1940

"Stood to" again. Pretty cold this morning. "Spotter" came over again at 4.30am. Started getting a bit deeper into Mother Earth ready for his mates to come. They come alright. 1017 bombers and fighters. Quite sticky while it lasted. The village that WAS in our rear, just ISN'T now. Fighters began to machine gun the main road. What a mess, be glad when night comes.

MAY 19, 1940

2:45am. Hell of a bang. They have blown the bridge up. He must be advancing again. Shells all over the place. Just in front of our position. Hope when he lifts he goes well over our heads. Lots of dud shells coming. Went to see the bridge at 9:30am. Lots of dead there, must have gone up with it. Took a chance in between shells and dived into café. Got a bottle of rum and two bottles of Vin Rouge. Didn't stay long. Good job as café went west five minutes later. Direct hit. Shells are giving us some stick now. 12 noon. Afraid we shall have to retire soon. Can't hold tanks with rifles and Bren guns. 4pm. We HAVE to hold on till 8pm and then retire. Roll on. It's been hell all day. Air battles have been worth looking at though. Got out at 8pm and marched 6 kilometres and got some lorries. Arrived at small village at 3am.

MAY 31, 1940 – MISS FLORENCE SPEED

Precautions in the event of invasion are detailed here by Miss Florence Speed, a middle-aged Londoner.

Signposts are being removed as they would be helpful to parachutists and the AA and RAC motoring organisations with their excellent road scouts have been put at the disposal of the Govt. Holidays have been cancelled and all the war industries are working night and day on a 7 hour week. Output has already increased.

For weeks now, the iron railings round bits of green in the parks have been taken down to go into the smelting pot. Those in St James's Park have nearly all been moved and I hope they never go back, it is such a great improvement. The lupins and irises are at their best and to have an unbroken view of them adds to one's enjoyment.

MAY – JUNE 1940

– SERGEANT L.D. PEXTON

Sergeant Pexton is captured on May 20, 1940, and is forced to march to a prisoner-of-war camp in Germany.

MAY 31, 1940

Many happy returns of the day Ena. Suppose my good luck will begin today on your birthday.

THE OIL-COVERED BODY OF A BRITISH SOLDIER WASHED ONTO THE DUNKIRK BEACH. THIS PICTURE WAS TAKEN BY HERMANN WEPER, A GERMAN TROOP COMMANDER AND WIRELESS OPERATOR.

Have had nothing but bad luck since my own, unless being alive is lucky. Left here at 9am and marched 20 kilometres to this village. Got ladleful of soup on arrival. Very weak. May get some more later. Don't know name of this place yet. Don't suppose we shall get any more food now, until tomorrow. Hope Ena has had news that I'm a prisoner, would be a good birthday present for her. Place called DOISCHE. No food.

JUNE 1, 1940

I'm about fed up of tramping round France and Belgium. My boots are very bad, got some small ladle full of "coffee" to march out with. Nothing else. I'm as hungry as hell. If I didn't need what boots I have left to march in I'd eat them. Boys are trying to boil dandelions and nettles to make soup. Hope it works. Stayed the night here. Dandys went down alright but bitter. Sick afterwards.

JUNE 5, 1940

Left ST PIERRE at 5:30am. Longest march yet and arrived here at 6pm. Got nothing on marching out Place called BERTRIX. Marched about 43 kilometres. "Lost 3 mates" during the march.

JUNE 6, 1940

Left Bertrix at 3pm by rail after the first really good dixy of soup. Arrived LUXEMBURG 9:30pm. Only stayed half hour and went on to place called TRIER. Climbed the big hill into concentration camp. We're just in Germany now. 3am.

JUNE 9, 1940

Yes this is our home camp alright. Getting treat a lot better now, better and more food today.

JUNE 11, 1940

Got our number today. 8806 is my new number. This camp is called STALAG XXA (17) believe we shall go to work soon.

JUNE 16, 1940

Wrote home today. Could have wrote a book of "wants" but space didn't allow. Hope it don't take too long for an answer. I'm not gaining my strength back on this food. Can't get nearly enough to eat. Smokes are out of the question altogether. Tried smoking leaves off the trees but didn't work. What an awful experience. Roll on peace and let's get home.

JUNE 1, 1940 – MRS M. DINEEN

Mrs Dineen, evacuated to Eastbourne and then South Wales with her two young children, expresses her feelings of horror at the suffering of the troops awaiting evacuation from Dunkirk.

The newspapers are full of the remarkable evacuation of our troops from Dunkirk. It is indeed a miracle and we hope those left behind will come through alright. It is not possible for me to express in words the terrible time our brave men have been through as they waited on the beaches for a boat to take them to safety. How must they have felt as they waited and were bombed and shelled by the cruel Nazis?

JUNE 1940 – JACK TOOMEY

Jack Toomey writes this letter after the Dunkirk evacuation.

Well, it started and after two days and nights of constant "alert" and all clears, we drunk a bottle of rum and another of Cognac Biscuit to get some sleep, the air raid siren was in a church tower opposite and about twenty feet from our window. We were determined to sleep somehow. I was still drunk when I woke the next day. A day or so later we were in a chateau farmhouse affair when a dog fight developed about a thousand feet above us Messerschmidts [sic], Hurricanes and Spitfires were having a hell of a good time. I don't know who won, I was too busy dodging planes, bullets, and AA shrapnel. From that day onwards my tin hat stayed on my head – even in bed sometimes... Never look a dive-bomber in the face, Bill, cos if you do you can bet you sweet life things are going to hum pretty soon, but pray and pray hard and run, run like hell for the nearest ditches and dive into them. I got quite used to diving in the end...

Then came the order to move and rumour had it that we were making for Dunkirk... As dawn came up we found the main Dunkirk road...from there to the beaches and they were black with troops waiting to go aboard only there were no boats. They gave us a raid that lasted from dawn till dusk, about 17 hours. The fellows laid down on open beaches with the bombs falling alongside is lucky it was sand, it killed the effect of the bombs.

The following day dawn brake and we saw the most welcome sight of all about a dozen destroyers off the beaches and more coming up – boats of all shapes and sizes, barges, Skylarks, life-boats and yachts. I was scrounging for a drink, we hadn't had water for a fortnight it was too risky to drink and all we could get was champagne and wines... The last time I had anything to eat was about 3 days off...That evening we went aboard after make dash up the jetty to dodge shrapnel...We got aboard and started, there were about 800 of us on one small destroyer. The navy rallied round and dished out cocoa, tins of bully and loaves of new bread...the first bread we had for a fortnight... We got to Dover and climbed aboard a train, we were still scared to light cigarettes, a light on the beach meant a hail of bombs...at Reading we got out and shambled to the road outside it was about 8am and people just going to work stopped and stared, we must have looked a mob, none of us shaved or wash for a week, our uniform was ripped and torn, with blood and oil stains. One or two dears took one look at us and burst into tears. I don't blame them, I frightened myself when I looked into a mirror... I was scared stiff for three weeks (but) it was something I wouldn't want to have missed.

Still c'est la guerre
Chin, chin
Love to all
Jack

JUNE 12, 1940 – MISS JOAN STRANGE

Joan Strange, a single woman in her thirties,

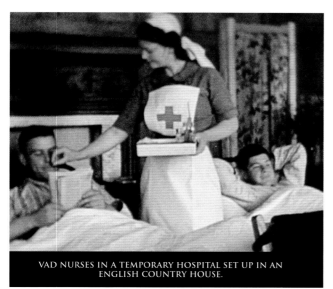

VAD NURSES IN A TEMPORARY HOSPITAL SET UP IN AN
ENGLISH COUNTRY HOUSE.

is hearing increasing reports of British casualties overseas.

The office says that in all probability all Germans and Austrians must leave Worthing before end of the week. Several of our hostels will have to close of course. The Germans are only 30 miles from Paris. Our RAF have got in first over Italy and have bombed many military and naval objectives. The RAF is magnificent. We heard of two local tragedies today. Young Lacey, married three weeks, has crashed and broken his back and other bones and young Blake is missing – he's left three babies (one set of twins) under two years. Mr Girdwood, the Congregational minister, is resigning, partly because of his extreme pacifism. I looked round the Public Art Gallery's War Photograph exhibition, which is really most wonderful. One photo I shall never forget "Home on Leave" – a small child rushing to her soldier father at the station with outstretched arms and so excited – very pathetic.

FRIDAY JUNE 21, 1940
– GEORGE WHITEFIELD KING

A law court shorthand writer in his fifties living in Sanderstead, Surrey, George King was a member of the LDV/Home Guard. His son, Cyril, was reported missing, and the diary takes the form of a long letter to him – presumably to be read on his return.

Just a few lines, Son, before I go on duty, so that our thoughts are together for a bit. It is a beautiful night – that's the worst of it, the weather doesn't fit at all with one's thoughts, or with what is going on everywhere. But, apart from that, the gardens want water badly, and Mr Gillet was moaning to me over the fence just now. Of course I keep the stuff going with the hose, but that doesn't make it grow.

Now, Sonner, as I have told you, this is my effort to keep a sort of diary for you, and maybe sometimes there won't be much in it, but when you come home it may help fill in some blanks... Recently I cycled down into the middle of Croydon to buy myself a pair of army boots, to which I have got used to again, so it has all come back to me. The only thing is that one gets a bit leg weary on patrol.

JULY 1940 – LEONARD MARSLAND GANDER
Marsland Gander worked as the radio

correspondent for the *Daily Telegraph* in London and at Angmering on the south coast, eventually becoming the world's first television correspondent. He was married with young children. While in Angmering, Marsland Gander volunteers for the Local Defence Volunteers.

JULY 2, 1940

This evening I went to local rifle range head-quarters of the Local Defence Volunteers the "Parashots", to offer my services as a week-ender or for digging trenches or anything else. I pointed out the difficulty that I might have to remove my family shortly. Nevertheless I was permitted to sign a form and told I might begin rifle practice when my enrolment had been approved by "Arundel" whatever that

meant. I was also allowed to inspect a rack of pre-war Lee Enfield rifles and told that there were fifteen uniforms among 150 volunteers! On the strength of my Bombay Light Horse experience I wanted to join the mounted section. I was told that it was hoped to supply them with revolvers but at present they had no arms. Our job it seems is to patrol the Downs o' nights and beware of rabbit holes. What we do if we observe the enemy I don't know but I conclude that like the Italian Fleet we "retire at high speed".

JULY 5/6, 1940

The whole place is bristling with Bren gun nests most ingeniously concealed. Generally the soldiers dig a deep round hole, make a circular parapet of sandbags and stick their tripod in the centre. Some of these nests have been installed in gardens. At one road junction, near the front, a small square hole has been cut in the bottom of a garden fence about 20 yards from the road. We saw three tin hatted heads apparently detached from their bodies regarding us through the gap behind the barrel of a Brenn gun. When patrols on the road stop and ask you for an identity card the three disembodied heads cover you with their gun. Not pleasant considering that the thing is loaded. A false move and you might be blown to rags. In another garden the soldiers have knocked a hole in the front wall being no respecters of property and use it as a loophole in the same way. Among the waist-high weeds on a plot at the end of Normandy Lane is yet another hornets' nest.

All the high bundles around the gardens on the sea front of the Willowhayne Estate have now been laid flat and the wind seeps through the neatly planted rose gardens and vegetable plots. Evidently the General intends to remove every vestige of cover. The soldiers since their experience of France & Belgium are terribly "Fifth Column" conscious, needlessly so I think, for I am sure there aren't any here.

I forgot to mention that my former acquaintance had a shotgun in the corner of his drawing room and told me that he is a Parashot.

Nor had he any scruples about using shot if ball ammunition is lacking.

The whole country is roused and in arms. These stout fellows will give the Jerries a

basinful – unless superior weapons beat them.

JULY 12, 1940 – MISS FLORENCE SPEED

Miss Florence Speed was indignant and incredulous at the official policy and suggestions regarding the curtailing of rumour-spreading; meanwhile, a neighbour has her own plans for dealing with the Invader.

When I saw "anti-gossip handkerchiefs" in a shop in Regent St – coloured squares with white borders on which were printed... "Just between you and me" I thought them stupid. Now Duff Cooper [Minister of Information] has started a "Silent Column" which seems equally childish. Rumours go round and round and it is to stop them that the Silent Column has been evolved. It sounds to me like saying, "Let's have a game together."

Silent Columnists are to be like the 3 monkeys – "hear no rumours, see no rumours and

CARELESS TALK COSTS LIVES

A POSTER AFFIRMING THE NEED TO
MAINTAIN SECRECY DURING WARTIME.

speak no rumours." No responsible adult should need to be told this. Yet the Govt must think the rumours serious to have to suggest such a thing. Silent C's are to ask the Chapter and Verse of any rumours they are told and it is suggested families should have Red Cross boxes and fine anyone passing on a rumour – it wouldn't work, not in this family!

Miss Sargood has worked out a plan for dealing with invaders – a pot of pepper! She always sees that it is on the table before she goes to bed at night. She has turned her brother's bedroom into a gas chamber – poor boy! – and equipment for this she has a syringe of disinfectant for purifying the air – this tool is put with the pepper pot as a tool of defence.

JULY 24, 1940
– STEVEN MELVILLE SCOTT WOODCOCK
Steven Woodcock was an engineer by profession, supervising the construction of the new Waterloo Bridge. He enrolled for ARP warden duty in May 1940 at Ladbroke Grove, West London.

The Wardens staged a practice "incident" at an empty house, 16 Lansdowne Crescent. It was good fun and proved instructive. Fourteen "casualties" of various sorts were distributed about the house, with myself labelled "unwounded". The idea was that if the warden who was dealing with the incident had any sense he would use me as an assistant. Longman was put in charge.

A determined friend of ours (Miss Smythe) was labelled "hysterical" and others were labelled with more or less serious injuries, one being supposed to have swallowed her false teeth. "Trapped casualties" were arranged in the basement amid a mix-up of old stores, fenders etc.

When the fun began the "hysterical" Miss Smythe made such a hullabaloo at a window that passers-by enquired anxiously what was wrong and Gwen who was passing was considerably startled. The attentions of the warden-in-charge only made for more shrieks and I wondered what Longman would do about it. However he dealt with her eventually and also with her companion, Miss Orpen, who was supposed to have swallowed her false teeth and got them stuck in her throat. His treatment for this was to lay her on her face and shake her head about, which made her feel so sick that she had to be taken into the garden and attended to.

Longman, a quiet (unless roused) publisher, flitted about in a cloak, bending over recumbent forms rather like a stage tenor searching for his true love in an opera scene. I kept passing him hints that there were three people in a bad way upstairs; and three more trapped in the basement but he seemed attached to the hall and ground floor rooms. I felt that I had saved his reputation by fetching walking cases from upstairs, including the aged General Adair who, with a pseudo-cut-hand, was holding it over an old bucket "to avoid damaging the carpet".

It was all very instructive and showed up our faults, but all the wounded were out of the house within half an hour and on the way to the First Aid Post or hospital, notwithstanding the "bomb-crater" at the front door.

WEDNESDAY AUGUST 7, 1940
– MRS GWLADYS COX

Mrs Cox notes the various salvage schemes and fire fighting precautions that were introduced early in the war in London.

We still await "The Great Invasion"! One of the latest Government leaflets to be slipped into the letter box is entitled "If the Invader Comes". The word "Invader" is printed in pale shadowy type, which seems in itself to proclaim the very shadow of its possibility. The gist of its official advice is "to stay put; not to believe, or spread rumour; not to tell any German anything; finally, to think before you act, but to think always of your country before you think of yourself."

It all seems very great and unreal that England, England itself, could possibly be invaded… Indeed the majority of us seem quite incapable of grasping it, but those on the coast have already come up against enough hostile air attacks in all conscience.

My friend living on the Sussex Coast, who has heard our aircraft roar off to the Continent, when Holland and Belgium were invaded, has been obliged to move inland.

While we await the worst frightfulness of the invader – Hitler had leaflets showered on us the other night, "His last appeal to Reason", we carry on quietly joining in various war efforts, such as anti-waste campaign with its slogan "Up Housewives and at 'em!" "Old love-letters can be turned into cartridge wads, meat bones into explosives, tin cans into tanks, garden tools into guns", Mr Herbert Morrison, the Minister of Supply, assures us –

"ploughshares into swords", in fact. So all kitchen waste, instead of being thrown pell-mell into the dustbin, is sorted into separate receptacles and carefully redistributed.

Amusing illustrated notices advertise this anti-waste campaign. The latest shows a brigade of housewives pelting Hitler & Co. (who crouch in fear) with old kitchen junk. Lord Beaverbrook's Aluminium Drive was so successful that after a few weeks, he was obliged to call a halt "to the generosity of the fine spirited, kind-hearted and patriotic members of the public who gave their pots and pans". It has been amusing to watch the growth of the local aluminium and metal dump, with its evicted treasures, varying from bits of a Zeppelin brought down in the last war, and old German military helmets, to ultra-Victorian objets d'art in bronze and copper and metal toys, all shortly to disappear in aircraft production.

One Sunday afternoon, recently, I attended an A.R.P. meeting for Housewives living in the immediate neighbourhood. Some thirty of us turned out, and sitting on deal benches in an empty house commandeered by the A.R.P, we listened to a talk by the energetic Chief Warden on how to help in, and after, an air raid, by promising to provide tea, hot water, cold water, blankets, hot bottles etc for casualties.

In connection with fire-fighting, stirrup pump teams have been formed. These pumps are each manned by three volunteers, one to fetch buckets of water, another to work the pump and a third to direct the spray. An incendiary bomb must not be tackled by a jet of water, but by fine spray, in order to prevent the fragments scattering.

SEPTEMBER 1, 1940 – MISS I H. GRANGER

Miss Granger, a young ex-teacher working in London for the Unemployment Assistance Board, finds her morale swings from low to high. Here she bemoans the waste of war, but celebrates the refusal to be ground down.

I think war against anyone is a beastly thing, I can feel a certain satisfaction that it is being waged against everyone: it will make the thoughtless think twice before they embark on adventures of this sort again or before they let things get to the pitch of its having to be endured by them again.

Up to now there has been too much heroic talk by some people about "giving" sons & young people in the cause of war. When it's brought home to the "givers" what it is like to be part of the great sacrificed I am not sorry. Civilisation, the thing that our own heritage can't be won by the few sacrificed: they must be jealously guarded, savagely protected by every single individual, & until that has dawned on us we shan't get or deserve these enduring delights: I almost begin to believe that people are slowly beginning to understand this: when they learn it and are prepared not to forget it this kind of holocaust won't break out again…

The raids are satisfactory; they show that the war has begun, the marvellous feats of the R.A.F. (I sound like Colonel Blimp, but it's true; the "never in the history of mankind has so much been owed by so many to so few"

[sic] of Churchill is the only way this can be summed up), the amazing courage of the people in the streets, are things to rejoice in. I do want to live till after the war if it can only be arranged, but since there must be a war I am happy to live dangerously in the midst of it, to risk the future. This war against civilians is a foul thing, but the wonderful thing about the present time is that it is a continuous proof that the only real factor causing bad relationships, confusion, bad faith is fear. For years we've all, or nearly all, as nations, as individuals been frightened. Frightened that, if we opposed frightening situations, bombs might fall on us, we should lose our wealth or position our chattels; our lives. And living in this mortal dread, we steadily began to lose all these things, & more: we lost almost everything worth having. And then gradually we have begun not to be frightened, to our surprise we can all see that we never need have feared anything at all. The bombs have fallen; most of us have lost a good deal – many have lost almost everything, but people aren't frightened any more. Terrors melt before a refusal to be frightened – I still loathe bombs, stuff my fingers in my ears when planes swoop low: it always seems, quite nonsensically, that they're seeking out my flat. But I think we are most of us not very frightened now most of the time: those dreadful years from '33–'39 when there was hardly a fear-free moment don't bear thinking of, compare very very unfavourably with this rather bomb ridden but satisfactorily comprehensible life we can lead now.

DAWN BREAKS OVER AN ALLIED CONVOY IN THE NORTH ATLANTIC. OVER 30,000 BRITISH MERCHANT SEAMEN WERE KILLED DURING WORLD WAR II.

SEPTEMBER 23, 1940 – MRS M. DINEEN

Mrs Dineen is horrified at the report of the sinking of an evacuee ship in the Battle of the Atlantic.

Today is fine and sunny but we hear very sad news. An evacuee ship, the "City of Benares", on its way to Canada with 90 children from England, is torpedoed in mid-Atlantic, 600 miles from land. We can hardly believe such a terrible thing has happened, but 83 of the 90 children are lost, 83 little souls who did not have one evil thought and who did not want to wage war with any man, and by Hitler's orders they are drowned…

This is the last [sic] German atrocity – the sinking of a mercy ship. What next will they do?

OCTOBER 1940 – CATHERINE M. PHIPPS

Nurse Kate Phipps has an encounter with the Home Guard.

As if one were taking part in a play where strange and unexpected things happen; one begins to wonder why one ever signed a contract with the producer of the show! Then we went out in the twilight and startled an owl which fled into a tree and squawked in an odd

SOLDIERS TRAINING ON A BRITISH BEACH, 1940: AFTER THE EVACUATION OF THE BEF FROM DUNKIRK TRAINING OF A NEW ARMY BEGAN THAT WOULD, ONE DAY, LAND AGAIN ON OCCUPIED TERRITORY.

way and blundered out again. To our surprise, we found the tree was occupied by a "watcher" complete with ARP telephone (or was it Home Guard)! Anyway we had a good laugh. Then the sentry (which was a new experience to me),

"Halt, who goes there?" (very fierce).

And we answered "friends" in the correct manner.

"Advance six paces and put up your hands" Well we did, but how awkward with handbag!

You were quite used to this sort of thing living as you do on a battle station, but I giggled. Well it turned out to be one of the men to whom you and Bazil so generously give baths, so all was ok! You may be interested in my remarks at this time. Such an absurd little sentry, his uniform and tin hat much too big for him. He seemed scared of his job, of the dark, of his big rifle. One could imagine him going home to a bullying wife and a houseful of oversized brats! But when we challenged he became another man. He was England standing at the frontiers of oppressed Europe saying to all tyrants "You shall not pass". And all that pass along this hill strewn with barbed wire and trenches, must stop, whether child or workman, housewife or King himself, at the word of this little man who holds life and death at the point of his long bayonet.

TUESDAY OCTOBER 1, 1940
– GEORGE WHITEFIELD KING
George King takes up the pen again, writing the diary to his son, Cyril.

I have not had a chance to put pen to paper since the last entries, Son, but now what news!! On Saturday morning there was an OHMS envelope on the mat, and I expected another letter about your pay, but, Boy, it was from the War Office, saying you are a prisoner. It shook me all to pieces for a bit, but I got straight on the phone to Northampton, telling the operator what my news was. She put me through in 2 minutes, and Mum must have known within 10 minutes of my opening the letter. Thank God, my Son, I feel 10 years younger, and it makes it so much easier to wagon every-thing else.

We have communicated straight away with the Red Cross, and hope you will receive a food parcel soon. Our hope now is that things will not be too hard for you, and our pleasant knowledge is that you will be out of the fighting which I am afraid must inevitably take place next Spring. So I will continue this sort of diary Son, but now it will be more in the way of information as to events, because I shall be able to post you a few lines now and again.

Well the only news of that sort is that the Air Force are still hammering at the "Invasion Ports" making invasion less possible. Those grand pilots have saved us!

DECEMBER 23, 1940
SPECIAL ORDER OF THE DAY by Colonel D.C. Crombie, C.B.E. Commanding 5th (Bideford) Battalion, Devon Home Guard

To All Ranks,

This is to convey to you my best wishes for Christmas and the New Year. We have certain grounds for congratulating ourselves. Half the trying autumn-winter season is behind us. We have generally managed to keep our tempers and the Battalion has emerged so far unscathed by Hitler's War of Nerves. And now the shortest day is past. The Black-out time will gradually get shorter and shorter and the amenities of life will improve from day to day.

But there is no room for self-complacency. It is true that, in pursuing our traditional strategy of striking at the enemy's extremities – where he is weakest – we have gained remarkable success. But for this very reason we must be on our guard. The enemy is conscious that with every day that passes our military strength increases. He is bound to try to achieve a rapid decision by attacking once more our main citadel – Britain herself.

The enemy must soon become desperate, and a desperate German is more tricky, more brutal and generally more disgusting, if that is possible, than oneho is successfully carrying all before him.

At what time the attack will be launched and whether it will take the form of an air "blitz" alone, or combined with invasion from the sea is uncertain. But come it will.

With the absence of our main striking forces overseas the role and responsibilities of the Home Guard are greater than before. I therefore call upon all ranks to fit themselves for the great task which is entrusted to us. In other words – to descend from the sublime to the commonplace – I appeal to you to intensify your training and to make attendances at training parades larger than ever.

It is up to us to hold the fort, to defend the Ancient Castle which for centuries has resisted all assaults of the enemy. The battlements are manned, the portcullis is down, the drawbridge is up, and I give you as your motto for the coming year

"Look to your moat."

JUNE 29, 1941 – MISS M.E. ALLAN

Miss Mary Eleanor Allan was born in Glasgow in 1909. During the war she worked as a reporter for the *Daily Herald* newspaper. Her letters were written to a woman friend in Scotland. As a newspaper reporter, one of Miss Allan's assignments is to watch a Home Guard exercise in London.

I have been watching the Home Guard catching German parachutists! Ah, thank goodness, only "exercise" ones. It was the weirdest thing I ever saw – a mock invasion staged among the desolate brick and rubble and ruins of what was once the world's busiest spot...

Today the sun shone down on this queer London corner peopled with troops in khaki. The steel-hatted men were "enemy" troops; the forage cap men "ours". Objective of the parachutists was to capture the telephone exchange. It was very eerie to see the steel hats creeping towards their goal, crawling belly to the ground, swarming like ants over debris and on to rooftops, while the defenders kept up a snap of rifle fire and threw grenades – balloons filled with water. Half bricks were used for grenades, too. Fortunately there were only 7 minor casualties. Battle commenced at 10.00 hours and finished at half past noon. Fortunately, we won.

1942 – ERIC RAWLINGS

Eric Rawlings, was 21-year-old wireless operator air gunner from Muswell Hill, North London. He was based with the 150 Squadron at Snaith, Yorkshire. This undated letter addressed to his family was entrusted to his brother Norman to give to his parents, Lillian and Frank, in the event of his death. Eric Rawlings died at the age of 21, during action with the RAF on the night of February 21–2,

AN RAF BOMBER NAVIGATOR.

1942, and was buried in Lincolnshire.

Dearest Folks

Now that I'm on operational work, and admitting that the risk is fairly considerable, I thought I would just put a few words on paper which you could keep as a remembrance in case anything should happen to me.

In the revoltingly chaotic world to-day where everyone is fighting and killing everyone else, it has always been wonderful just to take my thoughts from worldly beastliness and to think of the things which I revere and esteem most in the world – my family and my home. Love is such a very difficult thing to express here and now on paper, but I only hope that I've made you all understand and realize the depth of my love and the gratitude for everything which you have done for me.

Whenever there's fighting going on anywhere, you can always hear the words from people not involved – "Half of them don't know what they're fighting about anyway". Which is usually true. Well. I know what I am fighting for. I'm fighting so that in the future people will have the chance to live as happily as we all did together before the war without interference. Where the young 'uns like myself could make the most of the marvellous opportunities which you gave me for 20 years and for which I know you made many sacrifices. God bless you all, and may everything turn out right in the end.

God bless you all again,

Your adoring son and "Little One".

A SPITFIRE AND HURRICANE IN FLIGHT: ALMOST 23,000 SPITFIRES AND OVER 14,000 HURRICANES WERE CONSTRUCTED.

CHAPTER IV

WAR FROM THE SKIES

To the wonder of military strategists and even amateur historians, Hitler did not invade in the summer of 1940. Did he overestimate the strength of the Royal Navy? Did he still hold out for an alliance with Britain? Did his obsession with the defeat of Bolshevism get the better of him? Did his maniacal passion to rid Europe of the Jews overwhelm him? All these factors clearly contributed to his indecision. He didn't seem to know his own mind even at the beginning of July.

Operation Sea Lion, the invasion of Britain, was set for, "sometime after the middle of August." In the meantime, he put out peace feelers and began what he assumed would be the systematic destruction of the Royal Air Force. The first course of action was rejected out of hand, the second was a close run thing.

Despite some embroidery about numbers current at the time, the Luftwaffe and the RAF had roughly equal strengths at the beginning of the Battle of Britain. The RAF's biggest problem was replacing pilots, but the longer the battle went on the more likely it was that the RAF would prevail. British pilots who were shot down, exhausted, or even wounded, could and would return to the fray, often several times a day. German pilots either fell into British hands, or had to return to German territory. Sooner or later, Britain's increasing production of aircraft would begin to tell. September 15 has become Battle of Britain Day. On that day in 1940, 230 bombers and 700 fighters targeted London. Perhaps apocryphally, it was said that every serviceable RAF fighter went up after them. In any case a new legend was born.

German losses were colossal and Hitler realized that in such a battle of attrition, the RAF was the only likely winner. Significantly, Churchill had earlier ordered Bomber Command to attack Berlin, after bombs had begun to be dropped on London. This had clearly infuriated Hitler and the war of attrition was soon to be waged between the civilian inhabitants of the cities, not the airmen of the aerodromes.

Another Churchillian masterpiece flowed about the young men – British and from many other nationalities – who had fought in the skies:

> *"Never in the field of human conflict has so much
> been owed by so many to so few."*

The beautiful economy of the simple words "many" and "few" was irresistible and compelling. But "few" was also misleading, because, as Churchill knew only too well, it was now increasingly

TOP: AN RAF BOMBER CREW PLOT A COURSE FOR A MISSION, 1942.
ABOVE: 4000LB BLAST BOMB PUSHED TOWARDS A WELLINGTON BOMBER OF 419 SQUADRON AT RAF MILDENHALL.

TOP: 3 STIRLING BOMBERS OF THE RAF FLY OVER THEIR BASE AT WATERBEACH WITH CAMBRIDGE IN THE BACKGROUND, 1942.
ABOVE: THE CREW OF A STIRLING BOMBER WALK FROM THEIR AIRCRAFT.

TOP: PICCADILLY CIRCUS, LIKE A NUMBER OF UNDERGROUND STATIONS, BECAME A TEMPORARY REFUGE FROM THE BLITZ FOR MANY LONDONERS.

obvious that for Britain to survive it had to become a legion not a few. The Battle of Britain was a triumph for the beginnings of Britain as a mobilized nation; a triumph for designers, engineers, technicians, radar operators, munitions workers and repair crew, as well as pilots; a triumph for men and women, civilians and servicemen, miners and farmers, young and old.

The next stage of the conflict illustrated the resolve of Britain at war much more obviously. Liverpool had been bombed at the end of August. The bombing of London began on August 23. Then, late in the afternoon of Saturday, September 7, at the end of a hot, sunny day, the systematic destruction of the East End of London began. Over 400 civilians were killed. Another 400 were killed the next night.

The Blitz became associated with London, but all Britain's cities suffered, as did many cities in Europe. Germany and Japan suffered worst of all. But London became the symbol of British resistance, even the symbol of the resistance of the Free World. As long as London held out, there was hope. That Londoners survived, along with their compatriots in Coventry, Liverpool, Bristol, Southampton and other British cities was through a combination of fortitude and cunning. Those whose resolve might have been an issue usually fled to the countryside during the worst attacks. Those who had to stay, or wanted to, found the will to endure.

People flocked to the shelters – and to the underground stations, despite the fact that they were initially prevented from using them. Conditions in the shelters varied from the appalling to the tolerable. Nevertheless, a new mythology developed based on a kernel of truth

– the "chirpy Cockney", sharing his jokes, his songs and his opinions with a well-to-do neighbour from the City, who in turn shared his woes and worries with his new, working-class companion. This new kind of dialogue has become an often documented aspect of Britain at war. It also heralded a new, more democratic Britain: healthy social debate, across class barriers, among evacuees and hosts, between new comrades in the Home Guard and those in the Armed Forces and volunteer services, and among those thrown together by force of circumstances (like those sheltering from the Blitz). Although this clearly happened and it did have a significant impact on British social attitudes, it didn't transform the nation overnight, nor was the outcome necessarily positive. Class differences and social attitudes were deeply entrenched, and frequently prejudices would be reinforced rather than broken down.

However, all too real were the horrors of aerial bombardment. The terrifying wail of the sirens, the arresting whistle and screech of the bombs through the air and the sickening thud of the impact, these were not mythology. Nor was the heat of the fires from incendiaries, and the many pungent smells of high explosives, gas and debris. Worst of all were the sight, sound and smell of death. Bodies littered the streets and had to be dug from rubble. Cries for help could be heard from demolished buildings. Sometimes shelters were hit, resulting in an awful death toll. Several underground stations were hit, including Balham, Bank and Marble Arch, killing many who were

AN AERIAL SCENE SHOWING THE BOMB DAMAGE SUSTAINED BY LONDON, 1945.

sheltering in them. Despite these incidents, tube stations and even the tracks themselves were popular, unofficial shelters. It is estimated that as many as 160,000 people sought refuge in the underground system at the height of the London Blitz. Many people set up home, or had permanent "pitches". People lived in the caves in Chislehurst in Kent and camped in Epping Forest.

Life in the shelters had two overriding characteristics: good humour, which far outweighed any social unpleasantness, and the dreadful reality of too many bodies in a confined space without sanitation and fresh air. But the often-told stories and the fond memories of Londoners "taking it" during the Blitz, focus on the *bonhomie*, rather than the squalor of the conditions. Impromptu sing-alongs, buskers and amateur entertainers brought the shelters a modicum of fun. People even travelled from shelter to shelter to see what was going on in them. However, although many thousands did use the tubes and many more the official public shelters, most people either slept in their beds, or in their Anderson shelters, in their own back gardens.

Besides the redoubtable civilian inhabitants of the cities, the other heroes were the men and women of the many services that had to either contend with the bombing or carry on their work in spite of it. The Air Raid Precautions (ARP) services, the Auxiliary and regular fire services, the medical services, the rescue workers, the bomb disposal teams, the transport workers and the countless voluntary services, like the Women's Voluntary Service, all produced a rich history of courage, fortitude and improvization.

Of Britain's other towns and cities perhaps the experience of Coventry gives the starkest illustration of the impact of aerial warfare. The city was the first to be the target for a new Luftwaffe tactic, where radio signals would first guide "pathfinders", which would drop incendiaries to set a city centre ablaze. They would be followed by heavy bombers, which would then unleash their massive bomb loads on the illuminated city. The devastation that this wrought on Coventry accounted for over a hundred acres of the city and the loss of over 500 lives. Almost 900 people were seriously injured. There were signs of severe shock and talk of the city being "finished". In many ways the effect was more powerful in a small city like Coventry, where destruction was much more evident, than in a metropolis like London where there were always havens of normality and familiarity. Bristol, Plymouth and Southampton later suffered fates similar to that of Coventry.

On December 29, 1940, London suffered what became known as the Second Fire of London. Over 1500 fires were started, mainly in

THE SKY IS COMPLETELY ILLUMINATED BY BURNING BUILDINGS
DURING A NIGHT OF "THE BLITZ".

1944: A CIVIL DEFENCE WARDEN SURVEYS BOMB DAMAGE IN HOLBORN.

THE BOMB DAMAGED AREA AROUND ST. PAUL'S CATHEDRAL.

the City. London seemed to be completely ablaze, with flames and smoke billowing high into the night sky. For once, the fire services couldn't cope and many fires simply burned themselves out. The next day brought one of the enduring images of the war, as St Paul's, which had – as if by a miracle – survived the attack, stood proudly amidst the rubble and smoke.

In fighting the fires of war in Britain, over 800 men and women lost their lives between 1939 and 1945, and many thousands were seriously injured. In a remarkable example of how Britain came to mobilize itself, the exigencies of war led to the creation of a National Fire Service to replace the hundreds of local organizations that existed before the war. The transformation was complete within a few months of being announced.

Although the "spirit of the Blitz" was resolute, public morale did suffer. Feedback from surveys like the famous Mass Observation Study and others reached the War Cabinet. There were frequent reports of demoralized people and even demoralized cities. Although reports of civil unrest in Liverpool were untrue, there was widespread disaffection aimed at what was thought to be an inept local authority. Reports suggested that morale was very low in Southampton. It was said people were "terrified" and "so scared as to be unable to know how to look after themselves". All of this was perfectly understandable. As was the more accurate version of the myth that people would "grin and bear it": it was much more that people were "grim and bore it". There was often little to grin about.

Perhaps it was real anxiety about the public reaction to a possible peace proposal that made the government so cagey about the sudden arrival of Rudolf Hess. Hess had flown himself to Scotland in May 1941 and landed close to the home of the Duke of Hamilton, whom he hoped would help him put a peace proposal to the government. Hess was Hitler's deputy and about as senior a Nazi as there was. But he was caught by the local Home Guard, and Churchill instructed that he be treated like a prisoner of war. The press was instructed not to mention his arrival, and the news broke only when German radio announced it and added that he was acting alone, that they disowned him, and that he was mentally ill. Even then, the press was told that no mention be made of a possible peace initiative. He spent the rest of his days in prison and died in Spandau jail in Berlin in 1987, at the age of 93.

DIARIES & LETTERS

AUGUST 20, 1940 – MISS FLORENCE SPEED

Miss Speed was a novelist living in London.

If nobody else is, the Chimps at the zoo seem to be getting a bit of fun out of the air raids! One of the wardens was at the zoo with his little girl on Sunday. They were caught in an alert. After the raid was over, the chimps began mimicking the wail of the sirens. It was so realistic that at first people pricked up their ears!

Just how grim things are is thrust upon you when you see the Tube Squatters. At 4:30 today when we reached the Oval, it was already crowded with men and women and children, camped out for the night. There is no reticence. The platform was already hot with the smell of humanity, so what it must be like at midnight, it is difficult to visualize.

Blankets, pillows, cushions, were all laid out and meals were in progress. There is a revolting litter of greasy paper and the Porters at the Oval seem to have salvaged about 100 milk bottles.

It is a ghastly thing that men and women are forced into such a refuge. There is no proper sanitation, it will create disease. The bedding they bring is already grimed with the dust from the ground.

As we came up the escalator, many more were going down and a North Country woman was saying, "Come in early, I say, and avoid a crush" – when she got below and saw how many others had had the same idea she must have had a bit of a shock.

SEPTEMBER 4, 1940 – MISS JOAN STRANGE

Joan Strange, living with her mother in Worthing, witnesses fighting closer to home.

We had a horrid air battle over Worthing today and eight raiders were brought down. I saw one come down and two men "bale out", but it's all too awful. I hate even writing about it. The USA announced she was giving us fifty destroyers immediately in exchange for the use of island bases belonging to us – most excellent. Hitler shouted to the world that his "patience" is now completely exhausted!

Ken visited the wounded German pilot

ATS GIRLS OPERATE A HEIGHT-FINDING DEVICE FOR A BATTERY OF 4.5-INCH AA GUNS, DECEMBER, 1942.

AMATEUR FILM-MAKER ROSIE NEWMAN'S RECORD OF THE LONDON BLITZ
AND THE WORK OF THE HEAVY RESCUE SQUADS IS UNIQUE.

knocked off the bike. A second bomb knocked me down again and the 3rd sent a brick onto my tin hat. I went to Holy Redeemer and Browning and I set to work on stirrup pumps as the coke had caught alight. Smoke from the coke was coming through the broken church window. The cries and groans were awful. God! Help them all – A 20 stone woman blocked the doorway and we couldn't get her up the stairs. This woman was Mrs A... Later we got her up with help from the police but she died. Some had got out via the back entrance and window. Thorpe was under the arch – I rolled him over and saw his face – God – he had none and what he had was a mess. All his limbs were broken and lay at horrible angles. I recognized him by his hair, uniform and ring on his hand. Did a bit of first aid and heaps of odd jobs – everybody was wonderful – accompanied and helped the dying. Other bombs fell in Oakley St, Upper Cheyne Row (5–7 dead under wreckage) Lawrence St (a man and woman

in Worthing Hospital and found him very appreciative.

SATURDAY SEPTEMBER 14, 1940
– MISS JOSEPHINE OAKMAN
Josephine Oakman was a food office worker and ARP warden in Chelsea during the Blitz. She was 39 in 1939 and unmarried. She kept a meticulous diary detailing the times and nature of raids and worked tirelessly to relieve many bomb casualties.

18.27: Bomb on Holy Redeemer. Got sent off by Bert Thorpe on bike patrol in Glebe Place and hardly got away when HE sailed through church window through crypt floor to cellar where it exploded against some strutting among 80 odd people. I got

SIR JOHN ANDERSON AFTER WHOM THE
AIR RAID SHELTER WAS NAMED.

were both severely injured in the basement of the house in Lawrence St.). Re the bomb near Moore Gardens – it fell near the train bridge and caused some casualties in the Street.

SEPT 14TH – 1940.

We took 12 dead and put them in the garden by the Kirk as it was getting dark. A man and woman wanted to go to hospital together so we got them on the same ambulance. The injured seemed endless. Later in the night the dead were moved in cars.

I think my heart broke this night over the sights I have seen today – the Goulding family. Father and daughter, finding their lost son Gerald whom I put in an Anderson shelter down the road and dressed his foot. He was hysterical and wanted to get away and let his family know he as alive. One must have a heart somehow and somewhere – and mine I think broke – The love of that family for one another is a great thing and an everlasting – it made me cry – I cannot forget it – we still worked at the Holy Redeemer.

Many pigeons are being found dead about the streets (or dying) and all bleeding from the mouth. We think they pick up fine glass in mistake for food and this causes haemorrhage. (There is a great deal of small chips and powdered glass that has not been swept up.)

BOMB DAMAGE IN LONDON: ON THE NIGHT OF MAY 10/11, 1941 1,436 PEOPLE WERE KILLED AND 1752 WERE INJURED BY GERMAN BOMBS.

WEDNESDAY OCTOBER 2, 1940
– MRS GWLADYS COX

After many bombing raids on London, Mrs Cox's flat receives a direct hit and suffers substantial damage.

The bottom of our world has dropped out! Last night, most of our home, together with the whole top floor of Lymington Mansions, was destroyed by incendiary bombs.

I am so dazed, so tired, so numb, I can hardly think...

Just as I had written the last words "I then" in my diary, there was a terrible crash quite close, to the east of us, making the building stagger. We sprang to our feet, dragged on overcoats, shut Bob in his basket, put out the lamps and stove. Almost immediately, the plunk, plunk, plunk of incendiary bombs was heard above, on our own roof!

The sound was different to anything in the

nature of a bomb I had heard before, almost soft, in comparison to the loud bangs and crashes to which we had become accustomed – firm, spaced, even, like the footfalls of some giant stepping mincingly over the tiles...

Those of us in the cellar, fearing we might be trapped, or flooded out by the A.F.S., decided to leave at once. So, with my arms full of as much as I could carry, as well as Bob in his basket, I, and the others, stumbled along in the dark and utter confusion to the area steps. Looking up the shaft to the sky, we saw tongues of flame streaming out of the Price's flat. Ralph then tried once more to get up to our flat, but was driven back by volumes of smoke pouring down the staircase. All was confusion now at the bottom of the area steps – wardens and fire-men shouting at each other and giving contradictory orders. One warden seemed annoyed we had left the cellar, and ordered us back, but we could not return, as water was already pouring down from the fire-hoses above.

We stumbled along, blindly, in the inky darkness over innumerable fire hoses, water swilling everywhere, our shoes wet through.

The road was becoming more crowded now, as bewildered people ran out of the flats. An old lady clutched my arm, "Oh do let me come with you! I've lost my family and I am so frightened." She clung to us, and, all together we groped our way to the brick A.R.P. street shelter at the top of Sumatra Road. Here, in the dark and cold, we found other occupants of Lymington Mansions.

We all fell on each others' necks, like ship-wrecked mariners meeting on a desert island.

When the firemen told us, bluntly, that no one would be allowed to return to the flats, we at last, realized that we were literally homeless...

I went along to the flat, climbing the stairs with difficulty. My neat and orderly home was a scene of indescribable desolation. The dining-room was completely burnt out, neither roof nor windows remained. Ralph's beautiful antique desk, which, besides our Marriage Certificate, Fire Insurance Policy, contained all the letters I had written to him from abroad, covering many years, not even the ashes remained; his hundreds of books, his chief hobby, collected during a life-time, were congealed black masses of cinders; hundreds of gramophone records had vanished into thin air. In the dining room, the roof had fallen in and what remained of the sodden furniture was covered with a shining layer of molten lead from the burning roof; the carpet was inches deep in a wet mixture of ceiling plaster and burnt rafters. As we wandered from room to room, each with gaping holes in the roof, our shoes squelched on the saturated carpets, from the large water-tank in the roof above my bed had burst and added its flood to that of the A.F.S.

Wanting my silver cigarette-case, which I had place, the night before, in a drawer, I found that it had disappeared. Under my bed, my trinket box was lying, open, its contents scattered over the wet carpet. It had been taken out of the dressing-table drawer, which had been forced, and everything of the least value removed. Ralph's room had been ransacked and most of his underclothing, as well as a gold watch, taken – all this the work of looters...it was pathetic to see the window boxes all aglow with geraniums

British Bombers now attack Germany a thousand at a time!

AN ARTIST'S IMPRESSION OF THE RAF'S MASS-
BOMBING CAMPAIGN OF GERMANY.

and petunias, just as if nothing had happened.

NOVEMBER 1940 – MISS VERA REID

Miss Vera Reid, a middle-aged Londoner, spends many nights in a local shelter.

Another bad night. But further off than usual as everybody slept. Too bad to go home though. Woke up suddenly and through an open door, saw a man lying on two upright chairs, his head propped against the wall, his feet and hands hanging down. The light was very dim but he was directly in my line of vision. He looked ghastly. I had to get up and go over to him. Then I saw that he was crying. Tears falling down his face. I took one of his hands and said I was going to make him more comfortable. Put another chair under his feet and my coat over him. He seized my hands and began to talk in a strangled whisper. I had to bend over him to hear what he said. Just disjointed sentences. "When I turned the corner the street was there. It was gone. It wasn't there. Nothing. If I had only known it wouldn't be there. But to find it gone. I can't bear it... She was all I had... No one knew... No one told me... When I went the street was gone... All of it. Nothing left.

I wiped his eyes and tucked him up. I was afraid he would collapse. And knew it was something for some reason he had to keep to himself. He was shaking all over. It must have been this that woke me. Robert G. has a flask. Shook him and asked for it. He does not talk. Gave the middle-aged man a drink. He kept turning his head and moaning. But at last he became quieter and was so pathetically grateful.

In the morning he was gone. Just my coat lying there.

NOVEMBER 1940
– MISS GLADYS ANNE HOLLINGSWORTH

While she was living and working in Coventry, Miss Hollingsworth kept a pocket diary. Here is a draft letter she scribbled at the back of it.

I am afraid we have had a few changes of experiences since I last wrote to you, as you are no doubt aware. I expect my news will be

MEAL-BREAKS GAVE WARTIME FACTORY WORKERS AN OPPORTUNITY TO SEE CONCERTS AND PROPAGANDA FILMS ENCOURAGING INCREASED OUTPUT AND GREATER AUSTERITY.

quite stale by the time it reaches you, but it will at least be direct.

I will give you a description of my own experience on the night of Nov 14th 1940 which I shall never forget, even if I live to be 100. I had arrived home from work, had tea & had just sat down with my knitting for the army, when the city sirens started. We all grabbed coats etc & I made a dive for our shelter.

We had just settled in amongst rugs, blankets and pillows when we heard the roar of planes, they sounded exactly overhead, it was a marvellous night, brilliant moonlight & cloudless sky. The next thing we saw through a small crack of our shelter door were scores of flares dropped by the raiders. Then we heard the loud whistling & explosions of bombs together with flashes & reports from our ground defences.

We crouched down to the bottom of our shelter, straining our ears to make certain no small fire bombs dropped on our house. Thousands of fire bombs showered all over our beautiful city apart from a few small areas. We really had a fine & clean city, considering the amount of industry carried on.

A small place absolutely burnt out. "A place for everything, everything in its place". The worst thing about it is peoples homes and churches, hospitals & theatres have been the most heavily hit. Thousands of people have left the city and there are people still going every minute.

It seems as though our shelter flew into the air and dropped back. We had fire bombs dropped in the garden, Dad got out with his tin hat on & he put them out with a shovel and sand.

We never expected to come out of our shelter alive. However we are all safe although very nervous. I was shaking all the next day. We are now going out to the country to sleep, but if you write the same address I expect I shall get it sooner or later. Everyone has taken it wonderfully well, although the casualties were numerous, notices are hang all over the place.

CHRISTMAS 1940
– WILLIAM BERNARD REGAN

Bill Regan, although third-generation Irish and born in Coventry, was a typical East Ender, living on the Isle of Dogs. He was a bricklayer and his wife, Vi, had a clerical position in the Admiralty, but also worked in a war canteen. When war began, Bill, with his background in construction, signed up in one of the rescue squads. The accounts were written at the time, often when he got home, just after completing a rescue mission. Bill has volunteered to work at his "depot" over the Christmas period. One day he receives a call at 1pm following a raid on Saunders Ness.

After all this time, there is no big stuff to be moved, just one big heap of small rubble and concrete, which has settled into a tight mass, and requires hand-work. George Jillings had worked in the building trade with me, and on occasions like this, when it was possible to work in many small groups, instead of one large group, we two tended to drift off on our own, we fitted well together. I had worked on the building of the school, so I knew the general lay-out, and decided we should work down into the long corridor that ran for almost the length of the building. There were no survivors after all this time, 3 months, so systematic clearance is called for. After an hour or so, George called me to help him with a doormat he had found, but could not pull clear. It was black, and of a thick curly texture, so I fished around it for a while, loosening the packed rubble, then George came back with [a] length of iron rod to prise it out. I told him it was a bloke, and I knew who he was, Warden Herbie Martin.

Meanwhile, everyone else had gathered in one spot, so we went over to find out why.

They had found two, and had sent for the Light Rescue to come and take them away, and

TOP: THE RUINED SHELL OF QUEEN'S HALL, LONDON, BOMBED IN MAY 1941.
ABOVE: THIS FILM STILL CAPTURES THE WORK OF THE CIVIL DEFENCE CORPS.

80 YARDS OF FABRIC WAS USED IN MAKING EACH PARACHUTE.
THIS FACTORY WAS PHOTOGRAPHED IN MAY 1944.

usual corpses. I know I would have belted the first one who handled them with disrespect, but nobody makes a move to shift them, and are just standing there, gawping.

I looked up at George, and I just said "Stretcher – blanket". Then I put my right arm under her shoulders, with her head resting against me, and the left arm under her knees, and so carried her up. I laid her on a stretcher. "You'll be comfortable now my dear". I did exactly the same with the other one. I stood up and waited for some smart Alec to make a snide remark, but nobody did. I cooled down a bit after I had smoked a cigarette. I wonder why I had been so angry?

while I watched, two more bodies were being uncovered. I know none of us are very happy having to handle corpses, and it shows. They have uncovered 2 young girls, about 18 years of age, quite unmarked, and looked as if they were asleep. I look around at the other men, and most of them looked shocked, and a bit sick: we had usually found bodies mutilated, and were usually lifted out by hands and feet and quickly got away. Major Brown sees one man being sick, so he fishes out a bottle of rum to be handed round.

By now, I am feeling a bit angry at the prospect of these two girls being lugged by their arms and legs, so I got down beside them, and they have obviously been in bed for the night. They both have only their knickers, and short petticoats on, and dry weather we have had, and the rubble packed /round them had preserved them. Their limbs were not even rigid. They were lifelike; I could not let them be handled like the

MAY 1941 – MISS GWYNETH THOMAS

Gwyneth Thomas was a nursing sister employed at Highgate Hospital in 1939–43 then as administrative sister at Lewisham between February 1943 and August 1945. Here, she describes the improbable arrival of Rudolf Hess.

Great excitement everywhere, except Germany. Hess has come over to England, or rather Scotland. A farm labourer captured him, at least he went out to the plane that crashed near his home, and saw who he thought to be just another German airman, but it proved to be Rudolph Hess, Hitler's Deputy. Now why has he come over here, right in the thick of the enemy? It still remains to be seen. He is no good either way; if he has flown from his leader, he is a traitor, otherwise it is another part of treachery, on their part, to try to trap us.

MAY 13, 1941 – MISS VERA REID

The London Blitz becomes worse and Miss Reid finds herself in the thick of it one night.

Fear. Paralysing physical fear. It grips you and you feel contaminated, unclean. The worst night so far of all... Stayed in bed as long as I could but it got too bad. While dressing it caught me. I'm always frightened and this was something different.

Horrible.

Then it began all over again. It's like a sinister vibration which shatters you to pieces inside. Was quite incapable of movement though I wanted to get away before othes were infected. Like a leper.

Incendiaries were falling like raindrops. We could hear people in the street shouting to one another.

Then suddenly a man laughed. A good hearty laugh with a touch of excitement and triumph in it. My congealed blood began to flow again. My heart melted with love for him, for everyone. Even for those chaps up in the brilliant sky. Perhaps they too had been frightened and would now find release from fear. That laugh was like a signal for soon afterwards a fireman knocked on the door and told us we had better get out as they thought the house would catch fire any minute and they could do nothing about it.

Outside the sky was brighter than daylight. Glowing red and orange. In the road way opposite us a gas main had burst and was sending a burst of light up to heaven. Clouds of smoke rolled across Gloucester Place in both directions. From my room you could see houses burning away on either side.

I felt new born and the beauty of the scene made me gasp. Beckenhall mansions was on fire from end to end and as we scuttled across Marylebone Road the roof fell in and a cascade of sparks and pieces of flaming material shot up. Like one of those set pieces we used to see at the Crystal Palace when we were children.

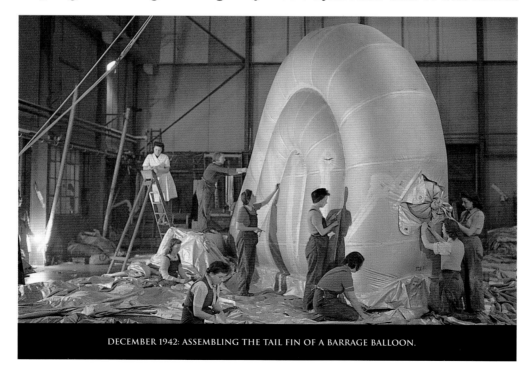

DECEMBER 1942: ASSEMBLING THE TAIL FIN OF A BARRAGE BALLOON.

The great full moon swung above against the bloody sky. The heat from the gas main and the burning houses was fierce... In the basement of the great national cash register it was like paradise. Soldiers coming and going, all dirty and unrecognizable but there were some cots and I fell asleep at once. The others talked in the distance...

By 5:30 it was quiet and although the all clear had not sounded we went back. No gas or water but we had left the bath full so I made tea for the firemen who were still working frantically to keep the fires from spreading. Had to use a zinc pail and all my tea. Sugar didn't go far but they were so grateful. That made me ashamed again for it's we who should be grateful to them. G. rang and asked if I would lunch with him at Claridge's and drive to Alto where D. was expecting us. Slept till 12.30. Couldn't wash as all water used by this time. No taxis buses all over the place. Houses smoking and the streets running with water. They were bringing out the bodies of some women which couldn't get near the front of the house...

Claridge's. Soft carpets. Waiters with cocktails. People washed and clean. George didn't seem to mind that I was grubby and untidy...

AUGUST 24, 1941 – MISS FLORENCE SPEED

Miss Speed, a middle-aged Londoner, cannot understand the mixed messages from officialdom regarding women and work.

What is wrong? For weeks the Press has been screaming that 50,000 women are wanted for war work, that women are shirkers. At the Labour Exchange this morning, May was told

they had 9,000 women on their books wanting Govt jobs and there are none to offer them. That is just one exchange! Thousands of women have been trained (at a cost of £100 a head) for munitions work for which no jobs can be found. Yet you read of women working 84 hours a week.

SUNDAY AUGUST 24, 1941
– MISS JOSEPHINE OAKMAN

Despite horrendous conditions, and being bombed out herself, Miss Oakman remained resolute in her positive attitude to her duties as an ARP warden.

A real lovely day.

We had now had a year since our blitz started in earnest last autumn – it had been a strange year and in many ways terrible one. I have learnt many things – things of what are really worth while in life. Material things seem to vanish like smoke in importance – it is better to have ones friends around than all the gold on the earth. The greatest thing is service – and being kind to others – to first help and serve and to look for no gain. I have lost friends, a home and possessions and yet I am still here. I have several times missed death by inches and I still remain. I want to see this war to the end – it is my one wish – and see all the terrors of cruelty of these air raids as things of the past – and see the beginnings of a lasting peace – which – God willing will endure!

HETTY SPEAR

Hetty Spear was a young mother, working in Bristol as a bus conductress. In these two undated letters to her husband, Gill, she describes the Blitz in Bristol.

Darling, you have no idea what little time I have, life isn't like it was when there wasn't such a thing as a Blitz. You see we have such a lot to do to get ready, the shelter has to be prepared every day whether they come or not, you never know what's going to happen. We pack our clothes each night as a ritual, so many people have woke to find themselves with nothing but what they've been wearing & now that the gas scare has started there is all that too, I mean food and water and first aid and umpteen things, I can tell you my dear, with my job and the house to keep straight, it's a big thing.

We had another Blitz here on Tuesday and another last night, so with the first Sunday as well you can imagine what Bristol is like. Last night they got the Power Station and the GPO – you can tell what havoc THAT caused without all the other terrible things. Oh, my dear, you have no idea how awful it is to lie hours listening to the screaming bombs, guns and houses collapsing and burning. It's just hell. I don't mind dying but I do want to be with you, it wouldn't matter would it if we were together. Bristol is full of RE's pulling down the buildings that are just hanging, and helping generally. They are blowing up Victoria St and the main places because it's all so dangerous as it is. Oh, George's Brewery is gone, Robinson's, Marsden's, Rowland's, Adams' and numerous others I can't mention.

There is nothing left of Castle St, one side of Queen's Rd, all Park St, Holwell Rise, all around nearly every street houses wiped out, besides numerous public shelters, surface and underground. I don't know if we shall get another but if we do there won't be much to hurt, only people.

I haven't told you The News. We had a nose cap of a shell through our own roof on Tuesday, it fell right where you sleep and split your table in two. I was thankful it didn't go through the living room, you shall see it when you come home. I'm saving it as a memento (what a weight).

Well darling, cheers once more to God, bless you always. Heaps of love, Hetty.

GERMAN AIR RAIDS CAUSED THIS LONDON BUS TO MAKE AN UNEXPECTED STOP IN BALHAM HIGH STREET, LONDON, IN EARLY AUGUST, 1940.

NOVEMBER, 1942: THE PILOT OF A SPITFIRE MK IX OF 64 SQUADRON AT RAF FAIRLOP.

CHAPTER V

THE DARKEST HOUR

Although the aerial bombing would return with a vengeance, the worst of the attacks abated for a while as Hitler's focus of attention turned east. He had always wanted the "living space" of Russia for his "Thousand Year Reich". It was also the home of Soviet Bolshevism, the arch-enemy he was determined to crush. What's more, if he was to eradicate the Jews of Europe – his megalomaniac mission – he had to conquer the East.

It would prove to be his greatest miscalculation and lead directly to his downfall. But it would also be a terrible conflict, costing many millions of lives. The hatred and brutality it generated were as severe and vicious as any in history. Whilst the invasion of the Soviet Union, Operation Barbarossa, ostensibly took the pressure off Britain, the middle period of the war, from mid-1941 to late 1942, was, without doubt, Britain's darkest hour. Even Churchill's reputation suffered as the war intensified without even a dim prospect of victory. The Japanese attack on Pearl Harbor, in December 1941, turned a European war into a world war and brought another frightening adversary into the conflict.

At the beginning of the war, there had been the "guilty men" of Munich to blame for Britain's inadequacies; but Chamberlain had died in November 1940, and Lord Halifax had been sent to Washington as British ambassador in January 1941 after being replaced as Foreign Secretary by Anthony Eden. For some time, Churchill had had the supreme power he said he needed to lead Britain to victory, and things had got worse, not better. War on the domestic front was hard, slow and tedious. The constant bombing, rationing, making do, boredom and simple tired-ness were biting at the raw nerves of the people. News from the military front was all bad. Crete, Greece, North Africa and the Battle of the

AIR CHIEF MARSHAL SIR W SHOLTO DOUGLAS, COASTAL COMMAND
INSPECTS 16MM FILM SHOT ON A RECONNAISSANCE MISSION.

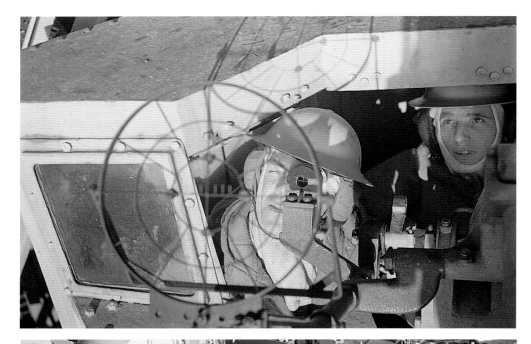

TOP & ABOVE: 1942: A GUN MOUNTING OF AN ANTI-AIRCRAFT POM-POM GUN ABOARD A ROYAL NAVY BATTLESHIP. THE GUNS WERE SO CALLED BECAUSE OF THE DISTINCTIVE SOUND MADE WHEN FIRED.

Atlantic all produced defeat, or grim news.

In the middle of 1941 German U-boats sank over 140 merchant ships, while air attacks accounted for another 180. The tonnage losses were increasing by at least 100,000 tons per month. Churchill ordered the figures to be kept secret. This stopped the overt bad news, but, equally, led to disquiet that the figures must be very bad if the government had to keep them secret. Crete was a catastrophe, where the not inconsiderable British forces succumbed to an airborne attack. 5,000 British troops were left behind after the withdrawal.

By the early part of 1942, people had begun to talk of Churchill's weaknesses, not his strengths. There was no one else to blame: he was too domineering, too eccentric; he drank too much. The maverick Churchill persona began to reappear in people's consciousness.

Serious questions were asked about the efficiency of the war economy. The Left wanted more state intervention and nationalization, the Right felt there had been far too much already. Party differences, which had been fairly dormant since the outbreak of war, began to surface again. Churchill's insistence on being both Prime Minister and Minister of Defence and thus in control of the war both domestically and militarily, was thought to be both too much of a burden. Some thought it to be verging on the dictatorial.

Although some relief had been brought by America's entry into the war, that had coincided with Japanese involvement. British losses in the Far East, especially the disaster of Singapore, added to the doom and gloom. Much of the criticism in 1942 was articulated around the need for a Second Front.

Heroic Soviet resistance to the German onslaught on the Eastern Front generated a huge wave

DECEMBER 7, 1941: BLACK SMOKE AND FLAMES POUR OUT OF A BATTLESHIP ON FIRE AT PEARL HARBOR, HAWAII AFTER A SURPRISE ATTACK BY JAPAN, WHICH BROUGHT AMERICA INTO WWII.

CHURCHILL CHATS WITH THE LORD MAYOR OF LONDON. HERBERT MORRISON AND ERNEST BEVIN EXCHANGE A FEW WORDS BEHIND HIS BACK DURING 1943.

of sympathy for the Soviet Union. It also intensified calls for an Allied invasion of Europe to help take the pressure off the Red Army. Membership of the British Communist Party increased dramatically during the year. In May 1942, a Second Front demonstration in Trafalgar Square was attended by 50,000 people. Churchill was in Washington discussing a Second Front in North Africa, not in Europe, when the news came through that was to represent the worst moment in the darkest hour of 1942.

The British garrison at Tobruk, in Libya, fell on June 21 1942; 33,000 survivors of the siege were taken prisoner. For Hitler, North Africa was a secondary theatre, but Churchill regarded it as vital. He was devastated.

When he returned from America, he faced a political crisis. The press was highly critical of the situation. It seemed like the Norwegian disaster all over again, which had brought the demise of Chamberlain. People said that they had done all that Churchill had asked of them, so why couldn't he bring them the victory he had promised? If the Red Army could hold the panzers, why couldn't the best of the British Army? At a by-election in Maldon, Essex, four days after the fall of Tobruk, an independent candidate, Tom Driberg, took a Conservative majority of eight thousand and turned it on its head to win by six thousand votes. A hastily prepared leaflet he'd circulated said, "Our sons and brothers fighting in far lands hang on desperately for munitions that don't turn up, while profiteers haggle with the government at home."

A motion of censure was tabled in the House of Commons proposing "no confidence in the central direction of the war". However, all Churchill's senior colleagues stood by him, particularly Clement Attlee and Ernest Bevin. This, despite the fact that Lord Beaverbrook had earlier made an overt suggestion to Bevin that the two of them might make a bid for the leadership, given the crisis that faced Churchill. To Bevin's enormous credit, he rejected Beaverbrook's machiavellian offer out of hand.

The great Welsh radical, Aneurin Bevan was the only significant speaker whose eloquent words could damage Churchill: "The Prime Minister wins debate after debate and loses battle after battle. The country is beginning to say that he fights debates like a war and the war like a debate." But Churchill responded with equal oratory, saying that if the Vote of Censure were defeated "A cheer will go up from every friend of Britain and every faithful servant of our cause and the knell

A 1944 CONCERT HELD AT THE ROYAL ALBERT HALL TO CELEBRATE THE 26TH ANNIVERSARY OF THE FORMATION OF THE SOVIET UNION'S RED ARMY.

of disappointment will ring in the ears of the tyrants we are striving to overthrow." He added, "the duty of the House of Commons is to sustain the government or to change the government. If it cannot change it, it should sustain it. There is no working middle course in wartime." Churchill got his political victory by 475 votes to 25. However, there were more than 30 abstentions. What he desperately needed was a military victory.

In September 1942 Churchill faced a thinly veiled leadership challenge from the one man who might have had the capacity to unseat him: the Labour politician, Sir Stafford Cripps. The German Army had reached Stalingrad. Churchill's new commander in North Africa, Bernard Montgomery, was about to face his first test against Rommel. Churchill and the entire war were at the brink. Defeat in North Africa would almost certainly have meant that Churchill would have had to offer his resignation.

Cripps had been brought into the government as leader of the House of Commons and, although he was not as popular as he had been, he still posed a threat as a possible successor. Cripps approached Churchill, expressing serious doubts about the morale of the nation and wanted the establishment of a War Planning Directorate to take some of the Prime Minister's responsibilities. Churchill refused. Cripps threatened resignation but was persuaded to hold back until the outcome of the impending battle in North Africa became clear. Much now rested on Montgomery's shoulders. Here was another maverick: unconventional and egotistical. But he believed in putting his troops, "in the picture" and treating them like grown men. They liked him for it and so did Churchill.

"Monty" launched his assault on October 23 at El Alamein. Despite total air superiority and superior numbers, the first attack went badly. But eventually, on November 4, the news came through that the Germans were in retreat in Egypt.

PRISONERS OF WAR, SOMEWHERE IN ENGLAND,
BRING IN THE HARVEST, 1942.

WINSTON CHURCHILL, WITH CHIEF OF THE IMPERIAL GENERAL STAFF, FIELD MARSHAL SIR ALAN BROOKE (LEFT), VISITS COMMANDER OF THE 21ST ARMY GROUP, GENERAL SIR BERNARD MONTGOMERY (RIGHT), AT MONTGOMERY'S MOBILE HQ IN NORMANDY, JUNE 12 1944.

THE VIEW THROUGH A TORPEDO TUBE OF HM SUBMARINE TRIBUNE. THE PHOTOGRAPH WAS TAKEN AS A PUBLICITY SHOT IN 1942 FOR THE BRITISH MINISTRY OF INFORMATION FILM "CLOSE QUARTERS".

Finally, Churchill had delivered. Montgomery became a national hero. Four days later Operation Torch, the Second Front Allied landings in Algeria and Morocco, began. Church bells, silenced throughout Britain since the beginning of the war, were rung. Churchill, as usual, got the words absolutely right: "Now this is not the end. It is not even the beginning of the end. But it is, perhaps, the end of the beginning."

Added to this particularly British victory was the even more strategically significant fact that the Red Army was not only holding its ground in Stalingrad, it was beginning to go onto the offensive. Given the crucially important American victory at the Battle of Midway earlier in the year, the Allies could at last see over the top of the huge mountain they had been climbing.

Sir Stafford Cripps left the War Cabinet and saw out the war at the Ministry of Aircraft Production.

DIARIES & LETTERS

FEBRUARY 1942 – MISS VERE HODGSON

Vere Hodgson came from Birmingham, but moved to London at the beginning of the war. She was a social worker in Notting Hill.

FEBRUARY 1, 1942

The news is awful. We seem to be at bay on all sides, and the Russians are the only ones who are ready and on top of themselves. They are doing spectacular things in the Crimea now and have relieved the pressure on Moscow and Leningrad. I hate the word Benghazi. Wretched place. We take it and rejoice and lose it the next minute. It seems Singapore will fall in a fortnight or less. As one MP said it cost 20 million to build and it won't last 20 weeks… Bought a spare hot water bottle in the week. They say we shall not be able to buy any for years, so thought I had better have one in store until we get Malaya back and the trees begin to grow again.

SUNDAY FEBRUARY 15, 1942

Singapore has fallen to the Japanese! It has been a mighty pleasant week for the British Empire – I don't think! We do seem to be biting the dust and no mistake. Everyone is mighty uneasy and no-one knows exactly what to do. Mr Churchill is to speak tonight at 9pm and perhaps he will give us back a little confidence, because at the moment we seem as near to zero as when France betrayed us.

TUESDAY FEBRUARY 17, 1942

Listened to Mr Churchill on Sunday night with bated breath. I hung on every word. He himself announced the fall of Singapore – a great British and Imperial military defeat. It seems that things have been far worse all the time than the most pessimistic of us ever thought! He told us that at no time have we been in a position to defend the Far East in a Japanese attack. That is why the Government had to put up with all their sauciness and been helpless. Yet we were lulled with the feeling of all those reinforcements sent to Malaya, and the poor men have availed nothing at all and vast numbers are now prisoners.

MAXIM LLOYD IMPERSONATES THE VOICE OF WINSTON CHURCHILL IN A PUPPET SHOW, AUGUST 1944.

TUESDAY JUNE 30, 1942
– MISS HELENA MOTT

In the summer of 1942, Helena Mott – a politically wary Londoner – is dismayed at the drop in morale.

The last day of June and sinfully appalling news to end the final six months of 1942. England has had nothing but reverse after reverse until one is afraid to open the papers. It isn't that one wants to hit when a man is down, it is a more serious and disheartening thing than that. We are beginning to feel the man may make no effort to get up again – lacks the vital spirit, nerve, willpower whatever it is in essence that fights for an ideal, with its back to the wall, it is not beaten in spite of tanks. Have we none of the spirit? Do we take on our duties so lightly that when the testing comes we fail? It is a horrifying thing for the thinking people of England to watch this decay of our will – of a once able people being rolled in the dust and losing its self respect and dignity.

COLLABORATION BETWEEN THE 8TH ARMY AND RAF IN NORTH AFRICA: SPITFIRES WERE USED TO SPOT ENEMY POSITIONS AND THEN DIRECT ARTILLERY FIRE. THIS PICTURE WAS TAKEN FOUR MILES FROM THE FRONT LINE IN SPRING, 1943.

BRITISH ARMY VICKERS VALENTINE TANKS MAKE THEIR WAY OVER SOME HILLY TERRAIN.

NOVEMBER 5, 1942

– MISS MOYRA CHARLTON

After a series of defeats, Miss Charlton, a Wren, is heartened as the war at last seems to be turning in favour of the Allies.

I woke this morning to hear Bruce Belfrage jubilantly declaring: "The 8th Army are advancing and the enemy is in full retreat all along the line."

It seems as if the tide has turned. Montgomery and Alexander, the R.A.F, and the 8th Army seem to have done the trick. Rommel is retreating in disorder to Sollum,

ceaselessly attacked by our aircraft. It really does appear to be the Thing at last. It must be hell for the Germans, and I must say I am glad of it. We've taken 9,000 prisoners already and losses are heavy on their side – and perhaps on ours? But it's terrific.

And Stalingrad holds fast.

I expect Halfya Pass will be the next stumbling block, but if we can stick the pace we should make a hash of the Boche.

Malta is playing a gallant part too in this battle.

Dad was so excited at breakfast that he consumed the whole of his butter ration (that was to last till Saturday) on two bits of toast!

FEBRUARY 16, 1943: CHURCHILL MEETS WITH GENERAL CHARLES DE GAULLE, LEADER OF THE FREE FRENCH, IN MARRAKESH, NORTH AFRICA.

NOVEMBER 11, 1942
– MISS FLORENCE SPEED

Miss Speed, a middle-aged Londoner, who published four novels during the war, comments on the rush of events in late 1942.

Armistice day of World War I. Celebrated by the Germans marching into unoccupied France thus breaking the armistice terms. And invading Tunisia with airborne troops and occupying Corsica – Italians with them. Events move hot and fast. De Gaulle broadcasts to his countrymen to resist the Germans and join the fighting French. French ships wirelessed to go to allied ports. Reports, reports, reports. The blood stirs. What next? One waits eagerly for news, news, news. Even the voices of the BBC announcers have a new timbre, sound jolted from their normal tonelessness and placidity.

NOVEMBER 15, 1942 – MISS I.H. GRANGER

After a series of defeats, Miss Granger, a young ex-teacher in London, is heartened by the long-awaited victory in North Africa.

Today we had church bells ring to celebrate the doings in North Africa – lights stalls were reminiscent of long ago, made me reflect. I am fond of the blackout in a way: I love the absence of glaring signs, advertisements, the sense of shape that it left – silhouettes of dark buildings & the restraint of the sky's lovely night colour, a thing we rarely enjoyed in sites before the war. But I miss lights in windows, friendly welcoming human elements. I shall be glad to see them again. As for church bells, I detest them. Generally in England they always sounded rather pompous & shrill – aloof.

Today, I don't know whether it was the good news or just an appetite whetted by long abstinence, but I rather enjoyed the bells this morning.

Later: just heard the 18:00 news. Church bells to ring on Sunday to celebrate our great victory in Egypt – How many bells are left to ring?

JUNE 14, 1943 – ANDREW WILSON

Andrew Wilson was the son of an Irish farming family from Donaghmore, County Tyrone and was training with the RAF at various airbases in the USA before he began flying in Bomber Command from the UK in May 1943. He was killed in action on June 11/12, 1943. Below is the letter of condolence from Wing Commander Donald Smith of 76 Squadron written to Andrew's father.

No 76 Squadron
Linton on Ouse
Yorks
June 14, 1943

Dear Mr Wilson

It was with utmost regret that I had to tele-graph you and tell you that your son, Sgt Andrew James Normandale Wilson, was missing from an operational trip against the enemy on the night of 11th/12th June 1943.

The target against which he and his crew were detailed was the heavily defended one of Dusseldorf. I am afraid that I can do no more than tell you that according to statistics of past losses, more men who are reported missing are prisoners-of-war than otherwise and at the very worst his chances of being safe are at least fifty-fifty. In the meantime, and until we receive any further news, I am afraid we can only wait and hope.

This was your son's third trip since joining the Squadron last month. In the short time he has been with us, he proved himself to be a very efficient and capable Captain of Aircraft, and a gallant member of a gallant crew. The news of his loss has indeed been received with the greatest sorrow.

SUMMER 1941: TRAINEE RAF PILOTS RELAX IN CLEWISTON, FLORIDA.

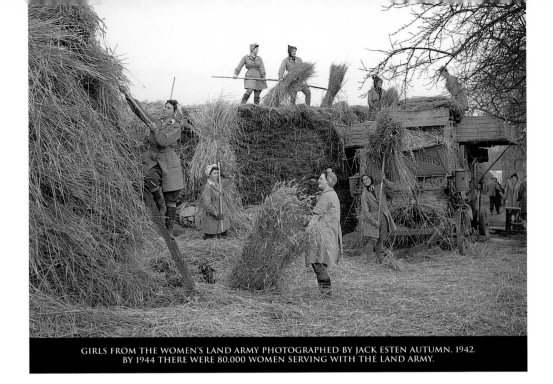

GIRLS FROM THE WOMEN'S LAND ARMY PHOTOGRAPHED BY JACK ESTEN AUTUMN, 1942.
BY 1944 THERE WERE 80,000 WOMEN SERVING WITH THE LAND ARMY.

If there is anything I can do to help you I hope you will not hesitate to get in touch with me. I can assure you that the moment we receive any further news I will immediately let you know, and in the meantime, please accept on behalf of myself and the entire squadron, our sincerest sympathy in these anxious days of waiting.

Yours very sincerely
Donald Smith
Wing Commander,
commanding
No 76 Squadron RAF

SEPTEMBER 14, 1943 – MISS PAMELA MOORE
Pamela Moore was a 19-year-old resident of Vauxhall, who joined the Women's Land Army in 1943. She was billeted at various places around Gloucestershire doing general farm work, which included a fair amount of spud picking and spraying. The letters are to her fiancé, Corrado Ruffoni, a conscientious objector of Italian parentage, who was himself doing labouring work in Wiltshire.

To start with had an awful night's sleep, two girls sneaked in very late "slightly merry", another one was up and down through the night sick, and not being used to sleeping on the floor, my shoulders ached. There are 7 of us in this great big hut, besides Beryl, Jane and myself, who have all cuddled together for warmth, there are two other girls, very nice, and you can guess what the other two are like. The greater part of the girls here are pretty awful, quite a number coming from Birmingham, but we three keep together as much as possible... Altogether there are 66 girls, in the charge of Lt Colonel (can't remember his name for the minute) but of course affectionately known as "The Colonel". He really is a nice old stick, and tries to keep the girls

BRITISH PARATROOPERS ON AN EXERCISE OVER ENGLAND IN PREPARATION FOR D-DAY ON APRIL 22, 1944.

WARTIME RESTRICTIONS ON UNNECESSARY TRAVEL LED TO A TEMPORARY RESTRUCTURING OF ENGLISH FOOTBALL. THE WIFE OF BATH CITY'S CHAIRMAN WASHES THE TEAM'S KIT, SEPTEMBER, 1943.

who are friends with each other together. He calls us with his whistle at 6:15 each morning, breakfast is from 7–7:45 and the lorries depart any time after that.

The lorry never came until 11 o'clock, having been ditched, and we started work, picking spuds. The farmer was a very decent chap and worked with us, probably to keep us on the job. We had a rotten lunch of rotten sandwiches and when it started to rain at 4:30pm we packed up work. This wasn't too bad for the first day, sort of broke my back in. but we walked most of the way back and then it started to RAIN. I got soaked to the skin. I've had a hot bath in a filthy bathtub, some half cold grub, can't find anywhere to hang my wet clothes here in the hut at the moment and it's not exactly a healthy state of air to sleep in. What a life!

OCTOBER 17, 1943 – **MISS PAMELA MOORE**
She moves to a mansion house at Oaklands Park, Newnham-on-Severn.

Saturday morning, had ever such a lovely time, stood talking with 3 Italian prisoners for most of the time. Monday we are working with a whole mob of them, as they won't work unless they have girls with them.'

MONDAY

My darling, what experiences I have had today, what food for thought! Why do I ponder so much on the ways and wherefores of mankind?

There was hardly any work done today and a day wasted bothers me. The mob of Italians were not wanted and only 3 came. We were stacking and hay-rich, 3 Italians, 3 girls, and then things started happening. Two in long kisses, and then the other 2 started larking about throwing hay which smothered the remaining Italian and myself. Hmm a good job I'm a little tough and have a few wits, anyway, Renee came to my rescue. I thought everything appalling and disgusting, yet how sorry for the fellows I feel, prisoners for nearly 3 years, a girl in a hay truck must be a very tempting proposition with no one around.

DECEMBER 19, 1943 – APRIL 4, 1944
– FLYING OFFICER REGINALD JACK FAYERS
Flying Officer Fayers of Ploughlane Dairy, Sudbury, Suffolk was an active member of RAF Bomber Command until he was shot down in November 1943. He was a POW in Stalag Luft 1. On arrival there he wrote to his wife, Phyl.

DECEMBER 19, 1943
Darling I'm so sorry about all this. My one worry

SEPTEMBER 1943: RAF HALIFAX BOMBER REAR-GUNNER JERRY VINES FIRES HIS TURRET GUNS AT NIGHT.

at the moment is that you and all at home are worrying yourselves sick about me. I can't stop you worrying until you receive this: but from then on you need have no fears. Physically, I got away with nothing worse than sprained ankles and a black eye. Spiritually I was hurt at first having to finish the war as a prisoner-of-war. But now I realize just how lucky I've come out of it all. The food at the moment is good and the company good-humoured. Conditions are quite satisfactory. In fact you don't have to worry about me at all. Just as soon as this war ends I'll be back with you darling: it's only like being posted abroad until then. Most of our comfort depends on the International Red Cross so will you do what you can through them. At the moment – I'm new here myself – I'm not sure of how much we can write. But I will write as often as possible of course. Look after yourself darling. And remember, this won't stop us or make any difference to us.

Yours always Reg.

JANUARY 22, 1944

Darling. I'm actually finding it hard to write to you. There's no news, except that the worry of

ROF WORKERS, NOVEMBER 1943: MAGAZINE SUITS OF FIRE-RESISTANT SERGE, RUBBER SOLED SHOES AND FIREPROOF COTTON TURBANS, SPECIAL CREAM TO AVOID ABSORPTION OF MERCURY AND OTHER TOXINS.

FINAL CHECKS ARE MADE ON DINGHIES FOR USE BY AIRCREW. DECEMBER, 1942.

being without you had made my moustache white on the left side only – & I'm afraid of each letter becoming a mere repetition of the order "don't worry". Last week I played soccer but my ankles are not yet strong. I can walk fast and for hours, however and my tummy is no disgrace yet conditioned remain good. I'm in need of nothing but a toothbrush and an airplane. I doubt if they'll send me the latter: but you could send me the toilet stuff. And darling don't let anything change will you? Keep our walks lovely, your hair dancing and your heart mostly mine: and sigh till I come: forever yours. Reg.

APRIL 4, 1944
Darling I'm feeling somewhat anxious for you

again. Please when you write, write at length about yourself and Sudbury and the Dairy. Sometimes it seems almost a dream-world, the one you are in. So, in your letters, do all you can to make it live again for me. Tell me of Quonna and Phil and Henry, the cows and the films, Cretia and Dad and Brundon: and get them all to write me, darling (except the cows). See you soon, forever yours, Reg.

APRIL 14, 1944 – MISS PAMELA MOORE
Landgirl Pamela Moore starts to consider the wider implications of the "working woman".

Well, I think you will have a very cushy job as husband in the future, for by the time I leave

1942: LOUISE SCHUURMAN, A FERRY PILOT, IN THE COCKPIT OF A WELLINGTON BOMBER.

the Land Army there won't be much that a man can do about the house that I can't also do. The last 2 days have seen me, with the rest of the mob, painting and varnishing the workshop here, with a paintbrush in my hand.

I was glad to read your opinion on the equal pay question, although I don't quite follow one of your arguments. One example of equal pay being a good idea is that of the bus conductresses. The trade union clearly states that they must have equal pay, so that when all the men on active service come back they will have their jobs, as the company won't be tempted to keep the women because they work at a cheaper rate of pay.

In theory, I certainly think a woman doing the same job as any single man should be entitled to the same wages. It would rather amuse me to see women independent of men, and, as

for a lower birth rate, I think there's quite enough people knocking about and what with the prospect of wars in which people only kill one another off – well.

OCTOBER 7, 1944 – PHYL FAYERS
Flying Officer Reg Fayer's wife Phyl wrote back to him, trying to conjure up scenes of their life together for her homesick husband.

OCTOBER 7, 1944
Reg my darling I have just seen the best film for months, it was "A Guy named Joe" with Spencer Tracy and Irene Dunne, I loved every minute of it. Darling how are you after all these months? Do you still look the same and talk the same? You will never really change will you? I wished so much that you were with me this morning, I was going down Church Street and saw the little boy – well I don't know what his name is but his mother was a girl Coles, remember the little boy we used to laugh at? Anyway this little kiddie was sitting on the edge of the path with a mouth organ nearly as big as himself trying to play it, and his expression darling! Well I've been laughing at the thought of it ever since. I should have loved to have been there, I miss you so much in the little things darling, things we used to argue over or laugh at, such as a rose-pink sky and a full moon which isn't round and dozens of other things, strange how they never go. Well my darling I'm on sleeping duty tonight so I must go, everyone sends their love and things are quite OK so don't worry will you?
All my love darling Phyl.

RAF CADETS IN SOUTH AFRICA WATCH A DEMONSTRATION OF TRADITIONAL DANCING BY ZULUS AT THE ROSE DEEP MINE, JOHANNESBURG, SEPTEMBER 2, 1943.

AN AMERICAN SERVICEMAN ARGUES WITH A CIVILIAN AT SPEAKERS CORNER, HYDE PARK LONDON 1944.

CHAPTER VI

FIGHTING FOR A NEW SOCIETY

As Churchill had so succinctly put it, although a turning point had been reached in late 1942, the war was far from over. The German and Japanese empires were only marginally curtailed and the key factor – the Allied superiority in men and resources – would take many months, and probably years, to grind down two fanatical enemies.

After much debate the Allied military strategy had become clear. Stalin didn't like it and it may well have prolonged the war by several months, but it was the least risky option. It was agreed that Germany was the primary objective, Japan secondary. North Africa would be the Second Front, and a subsequent attack would aim at Hitler's "soft underbelly" through Italy. Finally, the invasion of north-west Europe would come, but probably not until 1944. All this assumed that the Red Army would hold and even roll back the Germans on the Eastern Front. Similarly, American naval superiority in the Pacific would ensure no more Japanese expansion until the marines were ready to systematically destroy their empire.

This prolonged Grand Strategy meant that the pressures on the British war economy would be unremitting. By 1942, rationing, and the austerity that it meant, reached a peak. Almost everything was rationed. Although some things weren't rationed, like bread (although it would become so after the war) tobacco and beer, they were often hard to come by, especially during bombing campaigns and transport disruption. But taxation can be as powerful as rationing. For example, the duty on a barrel of beer increased from 24 shillings in 1939 to £7 at the end of the war: a six-fold increase. Petrol consumption was increasingly restricted: to 820,000 tons in 1940, 475,000 tons in 1942, and 300,000 tons in 1943.

Rationing was either based on fixed weekly quantities or graded on a points system. Grading allowed some consumer flexibility and also meant that the government could vary the allocation to reflect surpluses or shortages. Although rationing was irksome and caused resentment, generally it was understood and accepted, however reluctantly. Importantly, it served to keep inflation down. Government subsidies on certain goods also helped keep price inflation at bay. This in turn, reduced demands from employees for inflationary wage claims.

Following the rationing of a whole range of foodstuffs, clothing was rationed, as was soap and, finally, chocolate and sweets. By the middle of the war, there was little to look forward to to enliven the dreary staples of bread (the National Wheatmeal Loaf) and potatoes. The brown, National loaf was hated, especially as white bread was banned as "wasteful". Shortages of non-essential things were frequent. Finding things such as razor blades, cosmetics and vacuum flasks became very

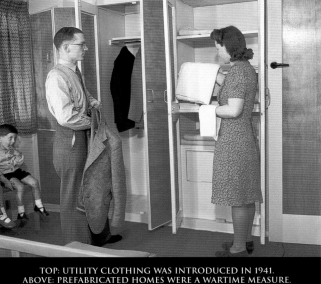

difficult. Similarly, getting things like bicycles, clocks and watches repaired became almost impossible.

There were some draconian, if logical, elements to the Austerity Regulations. Embroidery was severely restricted in the production of clothes. Only six styles were permitted in the manufacture of women's underwear. Trouser turn-ups and double shirt cuffs were prohibited in men's clothes. Shirts even had two inches of "tail" reduced and socks couldn't be longer than nine and a half inches!

Utility was the terrible twin of Austerity. Utility clothing and furniture was, again, a logical solution to shortages of textiles and timber. But it was also welcomed in that it introduced goods at prices that people could afford. On the other hand, national furniture production limited to 22 articles – each with a prescribed timber content, made of two qualities and three designs established by a committee – was a long way from the choice, quality and diversity that many people had been used to. For many people, austerity and utility were highly inconvenient burdens to carry. For others, a national diet, affordable reasonable quality clothes and furniture and full employ-ment were a distinct improvement in the quality of life they had enjoyed before.

The ominous dark side of austerity was profiteering and the Black Market. Both were extensive in Britain's war economy. Rumour and anecdote probably suggested that things were much worse than they actually were, but prosecutions did seem to be woefully inadequate. As was noted at the Maldon by-election, "profiteering" was a widespread talking point during the dark days of 1942. The government's problem was that, short of introducing the full apparatus of a police state, it was very difficult to stop. People often respond to restrictions by trying to avoid them and to austerity by trying to overcome it – by fair means or foul.

What the problem almost certainly produced was an even greater determination on the part of many people that the war would herald a new status quo in Britain, as soon as the fighting was over. This was certainly the position of the Labour Party. Its reward for loyalty would be a new society. The society created by the war effort was a model for their aspirations: high taxation, government intervention in the economy, a more egalitarian distribution of resources and a leadership highly mindful of the aspirations of the people. All that needed to happen was that when the German enemy was defeated, the newly mobilized resources would be directed at the enemy of inequality.

In December 1942 a blueprint for a new society was published. William Beveridge, an author and academic, had been chairing a committee to look at social insurance benefits. His report, Social Insurance and Allied Services, became known as the Beveridge Report and was a best-seller. Its central element was a universal social contract between all employees and the State. In exchange for compulsory contributions, all citizens would receive cradle-to-grave benefits. It meant family allowances, a national health service and presumed full employment. It met with a huge wave of popular support. The Labour Party welcomed it with arms stretched wide. The cool response of the Conservative Party would reap a bitter harvest in the general election that would have to come at the end of the war.

Another significant change instigated by the pressures of the war economy was a wider acceptance of women into the workforce and, concomitantly, at least some acknowledgement of their rights as individuals. However, the impact was slow to arrive. It wasn't until 1941 that Ernest Bevin, as Minister of Labour, acknowledged that the employment of large numbers of women was essential for the war effort. By 1943, women were conscripted into employment in the women's services, civil defence and munitions factories. At this point there were a million and a half more women in work than there had been in 1939. Significantly, many of these new jobs were in areas of traditional male employment, espe-

THIS "PATRIOTIC" BULLDOG, BOSWORTH QUEEN, RAISED £10,000 FOR THE WAR EFFORT.

cially in engineering. Although this trend was largely reversed after the war, one of the most marked changes it brought was in terms of the increased awareness among women themselves of their rights and opportunities. However, equal pay was denied to women, other than in certain specific instances and the issue was referred to a Royal Commission which didn't report until 1946. Even then, equal pay would be a long time coming.

As the war entered its fifth year, the British people had been living in a state of permanent mobilization and hardship for a very long time. On top of this, they had to endure serious military reversals and an intimidating bombing campaign aimed at destroying their means of livelihood and their morale.

But the British people responded remarkably well. There was little serious protest and disorder, and the nation stood together despite the hardships and the restrictions on civil liberties. Nevertheless, not all reactions to bombing had been calm and collected. There had been panic and hysteria and some looting. Not everyone had behaved themselves. The Black Market flourished, profiteering was rife and the crime rate increased significantly during the war. Also, although the people were united as a nation, differences of class did lead to old prejudices and practices being maintained or reinforced.

The final phase of the war, heralded by the invasion of Europe, began in 1944. As the Allied forces prepared for the massive invasion which would take the war back onto the soil of north-west Europe, Britain became an armed camp. Moreover, it was not an armed camp manned by men with familiar Anglo-Saxon and Celtic faces: it was replete with exotic uniforms, and faces to match, from every corner of the world. There were men from all over the Commonwealth, soldiers from the occupied countries of Europe, Chinese sailors, Russian merchant men, but, most of all, Americans – many of them black.

In all, there were nearly a million and a half foreign troops stationed in Britain at the beginning of 1944. The vast majority were Americans. This brought many problems, not the least of which was the fact that the American army brought with it its methods of racial segregation. The British found this perplexing at best, downright repugnant at worst.

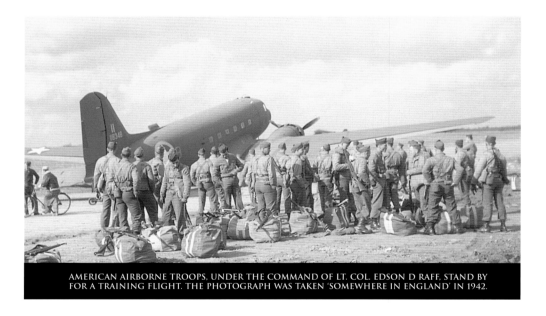

AMERICAN AIRBORNE TROOPS, UNDER THE COMMAND OF LT. COL. EDSON D RAFF, STAND BY FOR A TRAINING FLIGHT. THE PHOTOGRAPH WAS TAKEN 'SOMEWHERE IN ENGLAND' IN 1942.

The presence of the Americans caused both widespread fascination and resentment. They had everything from money to Hershey bars. They seemed ordered and disciplined; their military hardware seemed bigger and better too. They were also attractive to British women, many of whose men were stationed away from home, or who were prisoners of war. They looked and sounded just like men in the American movies. It is estimated that there were over 100,000 marriages between British women and foreign Allied servicemen during the war, 80,000 of them to Americans. Both long-term relationships like these, and short-term ones, didn't meet with much enthusiasm from British men. British soldiers' attitudes towards Americans, not always full of brotherly love at the best of times, were stereotyped along familiar lines: "They wait until the war is almost won, then they come over here with their cigarettes and nylons and chase our women around." To the ultimate annoyance of the vociferous critics, many of the women were happy to be caught!

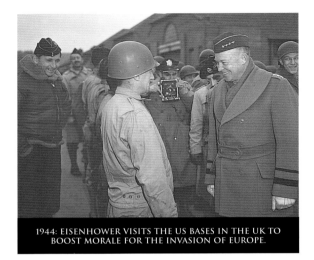

1944: EISENHOWER VISITS THE US BASES IN THE UK TO BOOST MORALE FOR THE INVASION OF EUROPE.

When D-Day came in June 1944 it was a monumental undertaking, a murderous fight to make a bridge-head and a terrible struggle to roll back the German army. But the Germans slowly gave ground in the West just as they were in the East. Similarly, the Americans on the Pacific Islands and British and Commonwealth troops on mainland Asia pushed back the Japanese army from its territorial conquests.

There were still dark moments to come, especially the horrors of the V1 bombing raids and the V2 rocket campaigns, but the war in Europe was over almost a year later, on May 8 1945. In the Far East, it was September 2. The death toll was at least 50 million. The world had been to the edge of the abyss. Freedom had survived by the skin of its teeth.

The last year of the war brought an almost unbearable realization of the price of victory. The evidence from the liberation of the death camps – both German and Japanese – and the stories of the terrors of occupation under Nazi and Japanese rule defied belief. The price paid by civilians everywhere, but in particular in the bombed cities and especially by the inhabitants of Hiroshima and Nagasaki, was without precedent.

In Britain, it was time to effect the changes that so many ordinary men and women had believed in for so long. Churchill was still loved, even revered. The nation knew what he'd done for them and would never forget. But love him as they did, he was a figure born of a different age. The nation wanted a fresh start. Angus Calder, whose splendid book, "The People's War", gives a marvellous account of Britain at war, relates an incident that perhaps summarizes the duality of emotions held by people about Churchill. Towards the end of Churchill's election tour of Scotland and the north of England in June 1945, he spoke in Glasgow at an open-air meeting, where people clambered up trees and on to rooftops to hear him. There were very few there who would vote for him, but they listened with rapt attention and applauded every word he said. When he went to leave the entire audience sang, "Will Ye No Come Back Again", a refrain composed originally for Bonnie Prince Charlie. This for an English Conservative Prime Minister, grandson of the Duke of Marlborough.

Now that the war was over, Churchill lost his antennae that allowed him to feel the mood of the people. His "Gestapo" speech in June 1945, where he likened life under the socialism of the Labour party to life under the police state of the Nazis, was not what the people wanted to hear about a

THE 1ST US INFANTRY DIVISION ON A PRE D-DAY EXERCISE IN WEYMOUTH HARBOUR. PROTECTION FROM AIR ATTACK
WAS GIVEN IN PART BY BARRAGE BALLOONS SUSPENDED ABOVE THE INVASION ARMADA.

new Britain.

Churchill lost the election, held on July 5. The results were announced on July 26. Labour won by a landslide with 399 seats; the Conservatives gained only 213.

The modern Welfare State did come as a consequence of the change wrought by war. Both successive Labour and Conservative governments, including a second Churchill administration in 1951, tried to implement the social and economic change that wartime Britain seemed to desire and deserve. With what degree of success, or permanence, is a matter for another text.

As for Churchill, rejected in the year of his triumph, as usual he found the right words. His doctor, Lord Moran, found him gloomy and morose in this bath on the afternoon of the election result. He suggested how ungrateful the people of Britain had been. Churchill replied, "Oh no, I wouldn't call it that. They have had a very hard time."

THE NEW LABOUR GOVERNMENT, ELECTED ON JULY 5, 1945, CONTAINED 21 FEMALE MPS.

JULY 22, 1944: WINSTON CHURCHILL, ACCOMPANIED BY GENERAL MONTGOMERY, VISITS MEN OF THE 50TH DIVISION AT CAEN WHO HAD TAKEN PART IN THE D-DAY LANDINGS.

DIARIES & LETTERS

APRIL 11, 1941 – MISS FLORENCE SPEED

Rationing begins to hit home, as Florence Speed, a middle-aged Londoner living in Streatham, discovers.

Shops sell out immediately they get their supplies in so goodness knows what the poor kids do. You can't get a 21/2d bar of chocolate anywhere. Milk chocolate is now illegal and Lipton's who used to have an extensive variety of sweets now only sell "fruit bars", a nasty sickly concoction and a "Nut Bar" which is a mixture of caramel and biscuit. Both 2d. A single apple today cost 41/2d!

The butcher's shop this morning had not even a chop to sell! There were a few anaemic looking sausages in the window and a couple of tins of corned beef. The shop was like Mother Hubbard's cupboard – bare. And like the poor dog we got nothing! So for dinner tomorrow we are going to have scrambled eggs on turnip tops.

FOOD RATIONING WAS INTRODUCED IN JANUARY, 1940 FOR BUTTER, SUGAR, BACON AND HAM.
RATION BOOKS HAD BEEN PRINTED IN PREPARATION FOR WAR IN 1938.

MAY 31, 1941 – MRS OLIVE COUZENS

Like most young women, Olive Couzens is upset by clothes rationing.

Fancy springing this rationing on us like that! I do think they might have given us a slight hint. You see, people haven't been bothering to lay in a stock of clothes – they have preferred to bank the money & draw out for the clothes when they were needed. Now no-one is reasonably equipped for Summer outfits – one doesn't start to buy until June – July. But I think the greatest blow is the rationing of corsets & bras. Not that this will affect me much, but to some poor women they are an absolute necessity & I think that it is an extremely bad policy to ration either of these goods. They are almost a essential to some as crutches to a cripple & no-one would think of denying cripples these…

66 coupons won't buy a complete Winter outfit let alone underclothes & Summer clothes! We shall have to start putting last year's top on the year before's bottom or else convert the drawing room curtains & cushion covers. By the time the war has finished my fur coat will be no more than a hide!

You know, you men are lucky. All our pleasures are being taken from us, our make-up, our perfume, our clothes & silk stockings, even our figure moulders, hair pins. In fact they will soon be asking us for our hair – everything that makes a woman's life worth living. I shall begin to feel bitter again. Fancy having to brave the Winter with no stockings. Brrr !

Darling, I simply can't write any more. My head's aching fit to bust! So with this painful

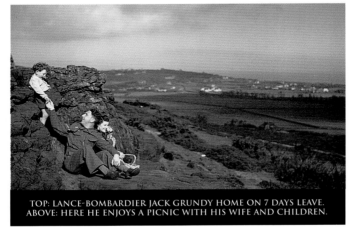

TOP: LANCE-BOMBARDIER JACK GRUNDY HOME ON 7 DAYS LEAVE.
ABOVE: HERE HE ENJOYS A PICNIC WITH HIS WIFE AND CHILDREN.

and sad ending, I leave you as ever

Your own

Sweetheart

JANUARY 6, 1942 – MISS E.M. BOLSTER

Maureen Bolster, from the Home Counties, was about 18 at the start of the war. The daughter of a deceased naval officer, she trained as a fashion designer. She worked as a billeting officer for a firm in Surrey before joining the WRNS. Her letters are to her fiancé, Eric Wells, an Australian in the RAF, posted to the Middle East. Here, Miss Bolster has very strong feelings about the promiscuous behaviour of some wives, while their husbands are away.

You know, I often wonder how many men in the forces have any idea how their loving wives behave in their absence. Most of the women, even the very young girls here seem to be married, but, my God, you'd never think so. Most of them seem to suffer from sex mania. There's one piece of work in the office who is married to a very decent lad in the navy – a jolly good type too. He often gets a bit of leave as he's on shore duties and while he's there she's all over him – "Darling Hugh, dearest love" and all the rest of it, clinging round him like a vine. He thinks she's heaven on earth. As soon as he's gone, however, she's out every night with one of the factory foremen and sits in the bus with him going to and from work holding hands. She makes no secret of it. She's been married four months and the foreman's a married man. It makes you think.

GRUNDY AT HIS LOCAL PUB. THE MILITARY CENSOR HAS SCRATCHED OUT HIS DIVISIONAL SYMBOL TO AVOID OFFERING THE ENEMY INTELLIGENCE INFORMATION.

AUGUST 17, 1943 – MISS E.M. BOLSTER

Maureen Bolster continues to despair about the reputation for promiscuity that British women are gaining.

Do you know what the Yanks are saying now?

They are saying that Englishwomen are the most immoral in the world. Nice, isn't it? And I'm really beginning to think it's true. Coming down in the train opposite me were an American army officer and an attractive, well-dressed girl of the upper classes. They were sitting hand in hand and talking about the hotel they'd been staying in. They didn't look in the least married. When she made a neat little joke about her husband being at sea and what the eye didn't see, I felt rather sick.

Marie Thornton met a young United States Army Air Corps officer in a train the other evening and he saw her to Ashley House where she was going to stay the night. As they said goodbye he asked, "Don't you want to sleep with me?" After Marie's strong answer he said, "I'm awfully sorry, only you see I've been over here a month now and you're the first girl I've met who hasn't wanted an affair."

MONDAY 1 NOVEMBER, 1943
– MISS HELENA MOTT

Helena Mott, an elderly Londoner, is disapproving of some salvage operations.

An amusing thing in our little town is the arrival of a fairly big grey limousine with a trailer (a square open cart) every Saturday morning to collect pig food from the bins placed at intervals down our road. The pigs surely should be proud that they are treated in no ordinary manner and that special care is given to the transit of their food and only the best means of conveyance employed. A limousine and the necessary gas, is often refused an earl, yet a pig may boast his rations are collected by one and the police do not ask to see the owners permit. Thus are times changed and every dog, or pig, rather, has his day.

NOVEMBER AND DECEMBER, 1943
– MRS M. DINEEN
By 1943, Mrs Dineen had been re-evacuated with her children to South Wales. She made several friends among the American troops who were stationed nearby.

NOVEMBER 12, 1943
While I have been in London, America has come to our parish… We have a social for 50 of them in school…and we all enjoy ourselves. They are very quiet and well-mannered and shy which is surprising to us and we cannot understand it. Afterwards we learned that the Colonel gave them a good lecture and threatened punishment if anyone did not behave… We are asked to invite them to supper on Sundays as that's a difficult day for them.

DECEMBER 26, 1943
Sunday Dec. 26th is a day of thrills for the children. All of them have been invited to the American Army Camp… The children's faces are a joy to see when they start away with cheers, and the Americans who came for them were jolly fellows who really enjoyed the trip… At 5.30 they arrived back after a grand afternoon. Each child had a packet of sweets, chocolate and gum, and then they told us of what happened. They each had a soldier companion and they went in to mess with him and had Spam sandwiches, doughnuts and peaches. Afterwards each one washing up their own plates. All the children had a great time.

TUESDAY AUGUST 27, 1944
– WILLIAM BERNARD REGAN
In 1942, after being literally bombed out, Mr

SEPTEMBER 1943: WAR WORKERS AND CONVALESCING WOUNDED TROOPS ON HOLIDAY IN CORNWALL.

and Mrs Regan moved to Beckenham, Kent. (Their children, Joan and little Vi, were already evacuated). Mr Regan quit the Civil Defence and resumed his job as a bricklayer, although he eventually went back into rescue work in the V1 and V2 attacks of 1944, but he found that morale had dwindled severely.

Home 6.25 a.m. Depot 8.5 a.m. To Dee St, to recover the bodies of 3 dead horses, and this while the Alert is still on. Our so-called superiors want dumping. Mobile canteen sent round at 11.30. Tried to sleep, unsuccessful. Wright doesn't sleep, neither does Pryor, Tuting, Brackin and several others. It's beginning to tell. Alerts on and off, all evening. To the "Tooke" 9.30, 2 pints, back 10.00; played 31s with Wright and Wenzel. I won 5d. To sleep before warning went again. Awake, to hear every bomb that came over. Sometimes five or six at once. Some sounded as though they were ours. Wenzel said he ducked beneath the blankets several times. Peculiarly, everyone is unanimous in their dislike of these things. They make a bigger mess than his bombs ever did. Some have a different note somewhat like an outsize bee, and they have a proportionate sting. Bill Brackin told me he dreaded night-fall; Wright and Pryor have said the same. There is not one man I know, who is getting used to it; if anything, it is getting everyone down. The sound of a motor far or near, brings everyone to their feet, with no exceptions. Not only is this so in the depot, but also in the streets. Kids playing happily, grown-ups going about their affairs; next minute, the streets clearing as if by magic.

You can see by their expressions, and the way they seem to go, – well, sort of, "let me get out of this". You can feel the uneasiness. Unlike the old days, when everyone waited to help everyone else.

JUNE 5–6, 1944 – FREDERICK WRIGHT
Frederick Wright's diary describes the Normandy landings as they happened before him.

JUNE 5, 1944
The sight at present is a sight worth seeing. Ships! Thousands of them, all loaded with Troops, Tanks, and thousands of tons of every other kind or war material.

We are at present anchored off Cowes, Southampton. A Parson has just come aboard to give us an address, and a few words of good cheer to enable us to keep up our spirits, for tonight, June 5th 1944, some thousands of Paratroops will drop somewhere near Havre

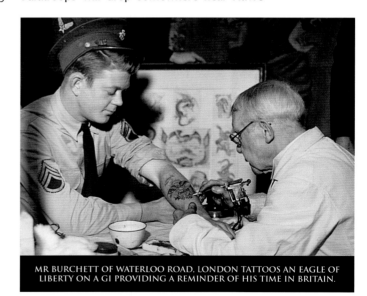

MR BURCHETT OF WATERLOO ROAD, LONDON TATTOOS AN EAGLE OF LIBERTY ON A GI PROVIDING A REMINDER OF HIS TIME IN BRITAIN.

ALLIED TROOPS WALK UP THE STEPS OF ST PETER'S IN ROME FOLLOWING THE LIBERATION OF JUNE 4, 1944.

GENERAL EISENHOWER STUDYING A MAP OF EUROPE WITH HIS
D-DAY COMMANDERS IN FEBRUARY 1944.

and Cherbourg. I think these names are correct, but it does not matter as we shall be there, all being well, tonight, midnight, for that is Zero hour. Some ten thousand planes will open up the second front. I am not a superman neither am I infallible, but with God's help, I will do my very best to write of what I see, and will write nothing but the truth.

TIME NOW 6.30PM

We have aboard our lovely fast steamship a lovely body of men – all in fine physical condition – Canadians – all in grand spirits, and all psychologically minded for they all know what they are going to France for. Tonight I shall be playing Dice with them, for that is their famous pastime.

TIME NOW 4.30AM

I don't think I have a wicked conscience, but blessed if I could sleep – I am writing in my sleep! Well here we are – the lads are all getting dressed in order to have a very early breakfast – just what the Doctor ordered – Roast Pork and Beans, Potatoes, Bread and Butter, and hot Tea!

TIME NOW 5.45AM

"Just like home" they are telling me – first real hot meal they have had for six weeks – been living on iron rations. God bless them all; someone's husband, son, or brother. They will land about 6.30am.

11.05PM, MONDAY JUNE 5, 1944.

Off steams the Armada! Three long columns of ships stretching from skyline to skyline – Canadians in middle columns – Americans portside and English on the starboard side. What a wonderful sight! Everybody on board in tip-top spirits such a lovely night – just like a pleasure trip. Not a sound – I could do with a pint!

By the way, we have far more to wear than Father Christmas! Something tells me personally, that nothing of importance will happen till we get there, so must wait till the fireworks start. I will write later.

Still steaming away into the lovely night. Quite four thousand landing craft will land in France within an hour or so – the excitement is now getting intense aboard. Yes! The French coast is actually in sight. The big battleships have opened up a heavy bombardment – the air is absolutely full of planes. I have just been up on our gun turret – a fine view from there. Our lads are all singing "You are my sunshine" – full of good spirits. I am just in time for a cup of Oxo – what a wonderful sight – the first to land – clear visibility. They have a big job to do; they must smash up all land communication and make a bridge way for the main invading force. Still the big battleships are banging away like Hell – off go our barges to return – We are all amazed! Cannot realize the truth – not one German plane to be seen. I can still see our invading barges, pitching and tossing, almost turning over. I bet a lot of them are seasick. Very rough sea – I feel right sorry for them. Poor lads! What a bad start – still – the right spirit is here.

TIME NOW 11.30AM JUNE 6, 1944

I can see our boats returning – now we shall get some news. What a sad sight! Yes! I am only human – I am crying like a baby! I can't help myself – What a terrible sight – our Sailor boys – only a few hours ago so full of life and spirits now laying at the bottom of the boat seriously wounded. My God! We can't pick up our boats – too rough. I see someone is having an anaesthetic! Poor lads! They have played their part only too well. We are now getting them aboard one by one! The Canadians have achieved their object; things are now in full swing! All I can see now are big ships loaded with tankers, bridges, and every other kind of war material making for the coast. We are lucky; we have only lost one boat.

TIME NOW 2.30PM

We have got our boats up and up comes the anchor. Off we go – back to jolly old England – good old Lord's Isle, and a good job done. Will write again when we reach England.

JUNE 7–9, 1944 – MISS E.M. BOLSTER

By 1944, Maureen Bolster is in the Wrens. She writes to her fiancé describing her experience of D-Day.

JUNE 7

My dearest…

I wish I could give you an impression of what the atmosphere has been here & still is. It's all something I wouldn't have missed for anything on earth… I expect this high excitement and

A SCENE FROM ROSIE NEWMAN'S FILM SHOWING BRITISH TOMMIES EMBARKING A TROOPSHIP FOR FRANCE.

tremendous tension will give way to bad temper and flatness when reaction sets in. It was impossible to work yesterday. We stood about, chatting, wondering, hungry for any scraps of news, hovering between wireless and windows!

Some poor things are frantic with worry over fiancés, boyfriends and brothers – nearly everyone feels anxiety for the men folk, we all know from here.

Planes have roared & roared overhead – great heavy bombers screaming south, other less noisy fighters. Few people slept well the night before or last night. It's all been such a tremendous thing.

I can't tell you what it was like to land back here on the eve of the 2nd Front – from home, where the war is something utterly remote and the village life goes on undisturbed in the tranquillity. It was a shattering experience!

It gives me an elated feeling…as if we've turned the most vital corner of the war – & there, ahead lies peace beyond the immediate battles…

all love Maureen.

JUNE 9

It's wonderful to see the men coming back, dirty, unshaven, some suffering from shock in varied degrees, others cheerful and wanting to get back. They all have tremendous tales to tell… On Wednesday night there was a dance here… I hadn't been there long when a young lad slipped into the hall and sat beside me. I took one look and I knew where he'd been. His eyes were bloodshot and red-rimmed and he was shaking like a leaf. He was just an ordinary seaman. Poor kid, all he could say was, "Make me forget it, please make me forget it"… He'd just had his nineteenth birthday… What that kid had seen was beyond telling. For one thing he had seen his special pals blown to pieces. By the end of the evening he could hardly stand for exhaustion.

THE US 1ST INFANTRY DIVISION ON A PRE D-DAY EXERCISE IN WEYMOUTH HARBOUR. THE LANDING CRAFT IN THE FOREGROUND ARE THE SMALLER BRITISH CRAFT (LCAS) THAT WERE USED IN THE INITIAL ASSAULT.

SOUTHAMPTON DOCKS, JUNE, 1944: ROSIE NEWMAN, CIRCUMVENTING SECURITY AND THE REMOVAL FROM SALE OF COLOUR FILM, CAPTURES BRITISH TROOPS WAITING TO EMBARK FOR NORMANDY.

JUNE 12, 1944 – MISS I.H. GRANGER

Miss Granger reflects on the D-Day invasion.

My dear, If you had been here last Monday night, in the early hours of Tuesday morning you wouldn't have slept much: the roar of the plane engines began soon after midnight, didn't abate until we felt deafened after 6 a.m. At about five o'clock I got up – they were flying so low & in such hordes, huge camouflaged planes with their bellies striped like wasps...

It was evident that it was either the best and biggest feint – or not, & thank God it wasn't...

So the past week has been a good one – there's no feeling among people here, least of all in my heart, of triumph, no salvoes of guns or bells ringing: it is all too terrifying, perhaps many of us are tireder even than we knew: anyway, even now the Dunkirk circle has been rounded off, there's no feeling of having got anywhere – but a profound relief that a new phase has begun. If the past few years can be called a "phase" it's good to have it at one's back, that is perhaps the only unblasphemous way of summing up 1940–44.

JULY, 1943: WING-COMMANDER GUY GIBSON WITH MEMBERS OF HIS DAMBUSTER CREW OF 617 SQUADRON: PILOT-OFFICER PM SPAFFORD, HIS BOMB AIMER; FLIGHT-LIEUTENANT REG HUTCHINSON, HIS WIRELESS OPERATOR; AND PILOT OFFICER GA DEERING AND FLIGHT OFFICER HT TAERUM, HIS TWO AIR GUNNERS.

JUNE 23, 1944 – CAPTAIN C.T. CROSS

Captain Christopher Cross of the 2nd Battalion Ox and Bucks light infantry writes to his family after landing via parachute in Normandy.

My dear Family

I have just changed my underclothes and washed my feet for the first time since I left England. What we would really like is some bread – getting awfully tired of these biscuits, but the army bakers are not here yet and the local French don't have any to spare.

My platoon is in very good form and we all get on very well together. The five new blokes

I had met shortly before we left are pretty good and with one exception fitted in well. The exception is now no longer with us – Jerry saw to that. But he has not dealt with us too severely – touch wood.

Being now at liberty to talk slightly about D.Day here you are for what is worth. For quite a long and very tedious time before the thing began we were cooped up very tightly in a tented camp opposite an operational aero-drome near Oxford. It was incredibly hot while we were there (Whitsun) but they stretched a point and allowed us out of camp to go across to the R.A.F. mess and have a bath. E.N.S.A. sent a show down one after-noon – held in plain air – quite amusing. And occasionally we packed a few sweaty men very tightly into a tent and showed them a film. But it was a trying time and a lot of money changed hands at cards. Meanwhile the officers and N.C.O.'s were very busy learning the story of what we were going to do, memorising maps, studying models, air photographs, intelligence reports and all that sort of thing. All done in the near nude in a Nissen hut, whose doors and windows had to be kept shut! And throughout this time about half the company were within a dozen miles of their homes and they had great temptations. However all was well. The whole business was a bit nerve-wracking though because we were not told exactly when D.Day was to be and then, when we were told, the whole thing was put off for a day just as we were about keyed up to go. The glider flight was bloody! It was, of course, longer than most we've done before because of the business of getting into

formation, collecting fighter escort and so on. After about an hour I began to be sick and continued until we were over the Channel where the air was much calmer. The Channel was a wonderful sight – especially the traffic at this end – Piccadilly Circus wasn't in it. We were not over the coast this side long enough for me to be sick again and we were pretty busy thinking about landing. The landing was ghastly. Mine was the first glider down though we were not quite in the right place, and the damn thing bucketed along a very upsy-downsy field for a bit and then broke across the middle – We just chopped through those anti-landing poles (like the ones I used to cut during my forestry vac.) as we went along. However the two halves of the glider fetched up very close together and we quickly got out ourselves and our equipment and lay down under the thing because other gliders were coming in all round and Jerries were shooting things about at them and us so it wasn't very healthy to wander about. Our immediate opposition – machine gun in a little trench – was very effectively silenced by another glider which fetched up plumb on the trench and a couple of Huns – quite terrified – came put with their hands up! Having discovered that we were all there and bound up a few scratches we then set off to the scene of the battle. I shall not tell you about that except that apart from a bar of chocolate and half the contents of my whisky flask I had no time to eat or drink for a very uncomfortably long time – too much else to do, but it seems incredible now. From my last meal in England to my first cup of char and hard ration in France was very nearly

48 hours! But I've been making up for it since.

The French people I have met have been marvellous, very pleased to see us – pleasure mingled with apprehension because they knew that when we arrived it might mean shelling, it might mean we should have to raid their houses to protect ourselves, it would assuredly mean the death of a lot of their live-stock. This is a horse and cattle-breeding district, and one of the saddest things is to see their carcasses lying about, nobody having time to deal with them – and fields full of very scared animals, some of them wounded. The local drink is cider – rough but very good and I hate to think what goes into the making of it. However the alcohol in it makes it safer to drink than the water hereabouts. The civilians used to give us cider if we asked for a drink. Recently though we have not been near any places with inhabitants about.

As I write a force of about 500 fortresses has just gone overhead – most encouraging. You probably have a very good idea of where I am and what I am doing from the newspapers. We get a few belated papers out here but only the *Herald* and *Mirror* variety and they sometimes give rather highly coloured accounts of our doings, though not always strictly accurately. We were rather annoyed when one of them said that it was parachutists who had captured and held the bridge over the Orne.

A very touching scene yesterday. I went back to revisit a farm I once occupied for a couple of days and where we made ourselves very popular and were very polite. They fell on my neck and called me "their own lieutenant" and were very pleased to see me because we behaved so much better than the people who took over from us – loaded me with vegetables, cabbage, carrots, onions and lettuce and would only accept a few cigarettes and a bit of tobacco in payment.

Love to you all, Chris

JUNE 23, 1944 – MISS I.H. GRANGER

A week after D-Day, the Germans launched V1 flying bombs against Britain. Miss Granger is tired of bombardment, but maintains her sense of humour.

My dear,

You may like to hear about the Nazis' new toy. I haven't time for a long letter, but in 1940–41 you were interested in our bombard-ments, anyway air raids get distorted and exaggerated in the press. (I am far less broad minded than that when the beastly things are humming about, inclined to feel that they aren't played up nearly enough! But that's in the early hours of the morning & is quite another story). For so long secret weapons have been promised by the Nazi High Command, now they have begun: this is in a way encouraging – again a thought more suitable to daylight and not one I endorse round about dawn.

What is difficult to determine is why (a) we all feel crosser (b) many of us feel distinctly more frightened than in an attack by ordinary planes... Probably it's an accumulation of rea-sons: we are tireder than in 1940, at my age I feel a lot more than four years older – hundreds of years tireder and older, a bit inclined to jump at bangs (this will stop I expect when my heart is well). Then a lady from Camden Town stated clearly the other day that it didn't seem fair not to shoot at a man: I don't think I mind that, though if it's a Nazi in the plane I like him to get wiped off before he can get me... This thing that goes bumbling & flying about is only metal, ideologically harmless. On the credit side there is the certainty that, once it's passed over your house (God knows how one decides this, but one always does!) it can't turn round & come back, hunt you out like a real bomber – but on the debit side is the irritating certainty that it doesn't do any good to bring it down (at any rate in London – the sea's the best grave for it), because it'll come down anyway and make a maddening mess when it does...

I hear the coastal defences are getting them under control well which is comfortable for us) you can hear them hammering their way along, usually one at a time. Just before they fall the engine seems to rev up and get very noisy, then it cuts right out and there's silence: that's the time to count, 5–15 seconds. So far my next feeling is of relief (if the bang is like a bursting paper bag) or of momentary terror if it's got the old-fashioned land-mine lilt to it. Then nothing more till the next one jumbles, bumbles over...

I was catching a bus when one fell two streets away from me the other day – I saw it coming, ducked (to no purpose – there was no need), it made its bursting noise, but as it's not a penetrating weapon you don't get the ground tremor of the ordinary bomb. The blast is nasty, it fairly tears windows & sashes to pieces...

There is the lighter side to this: when I saw one in the street hurtling down, a lady near by was holding a tin hat. For what seemed eternity, was probably a millionth of a second I wished I'd had the prudence to drag mine with me. She didn't put it on, but when the missile had exploded we looked at each other & laughed – she couldn't put it on as it had been used as a shopping basket & held her month's jam & sugar ration.

JULY 29, 1944 – MISS GWYNETH THOMAS
Gwyneth Thomas is now nursing at Lewisham Hospital, which receives a direct hit.

We had a few nights' peace from the flying bombs, and we had almost forgotten, but on 26th July we had a direct hit, on the medical block, next to our nurses' home where we were sleeping. The corridor walls next to the one I was in caved in, yet no one screamed, everyone was out of their bunks and in various cubby holes in a split second, all making for the wards that were by now blazing. The dispensary nearby was like a furnace, the medical superintendent's office next to it, the linen store, and sewing room, plus a room where there were thousands of records of patients, the Ration Book office, all blazing like fury. I had to stop in my way to the ward to attend to a maid who had been on the corridor. She had a deep laceration on her scalp. We packed her up with hot water bottles, covered her wounds, and then, after making sure she would be all right, left her in charge of two nurses and other maids who had escaped. I then got over to the wards. God knows how we got 200 patients out of that furnace; two were trapped, but were rescued just in time. A visitor was burned to death in the waiting room, and one nurse was buried, or rather, shot off by the falling masonry, where they found her four hours later – she was, of course, dead.

I could not fully describe the scene; by now, patients were first put on blankets on the ground, (on the drive) then later, when we were sure all had been rescued, we brought them over to the nurses' home, lined them up in the lecture rooms, sitting rooms, corridors, many old people, some paralysed, some dying from their various ills, not many injured. Three nurses were among those who were; one nurse had worked all through it with a severed artery, which she had had bound, the others with deep lacerations of legs, one with a head wound. If only I had the gift of writing, I should tell of many heroic deeds that morning – nursing staff trying to fight through to the patients they thought were trapped. Matron was marvellous as a head, she let her staff use their sense, and they did. I had always wondered how we would react if we did get a direct hit. God gave us superhuman courage and with it the strength to lift the helpless. So from dawn to dusk that day we worked and not until we stopped to get into our bunks at night did we feel the effects.

WEDNESDAY FEBRUARY 21, 1945
– GEORGE TEMPLE

George Temple was serving in the 19th Indian Division in Burma.

10649414 WO I G.P. TEMPLE,
HQRA 19 Ind Div, SEAC
My dear Jean,

The rabbit in his burrow keeps, no guarded watch – in peace he sleeps. The wolf that howls in challenging night, cowers to her lair in morning light, each little bird entwines a nest where she may lean her lovely breast, couched in the shadow of the bough, but thou, O man – what rest hast thou! Hence, for the last few weeks I have been emulating aforesaid rabbit, as far as is humanly possible to keep clear of the arrow that flieth by night (or its more modern counterpart – the flying bullet down the pass, that whistles clear, ALL FLESH IS GRASS.)

I think that is about enough for the present otherwise you will consider me smug and boring – I am introspective enough to realize that.

Well dear I trust that your recent bitter weather didn't treat Granny and your self too unkindly, the weather here has been just wonderful, which is just as well, considering the type of country through which we have had to operate, as you have no doubt read we are all thin red 'eroes now, but in actual fact I found it much more safe and congenial in Chesham than it is here. On the whole though it is a most interesting country and the quaint little places we pass though must have been rather pretty prior to the devastating advent of shot and shell, I have been in several of the temples and pagodas and the Burmans seem to erect one for each member of the community, the carvings are really masterpieces, and in the larger ones they have numerous figures of Buddha beautifully finished with gold leaf and what looks like a large diamond in the forehead (but I think they must be just a good crystal, or they would most probably have been looted here now) and all around the base are smaller ones that sparkle wonderfully when the sun strikes them, and just across the way from us is a larger temple with a huge stone sitting statue about twenty feet high, these people certainly take pains with their religion – pagan though it may be. More as a novelty and recreation than anything else is our daily bathe in the IRRAWADDY (the crocodiles seem to have forsaken this noisy part of the river for streamlets new) and today we took out one of the local boats but unfortunately it soon became apparent that something was amiss – the holes in the bottom wouldn't let the water out so after we had got out a little way it sunk to the gunnels and we had to swim alongside and push it back – we were all in swim suits, real or improvized, so you can imagine we had quite a laugh out of it.

Another funny sidelight on this otherwise unfunny existence occurred the other day – it was after two night of jitters with all manner of fireworks flying about throughout the night –

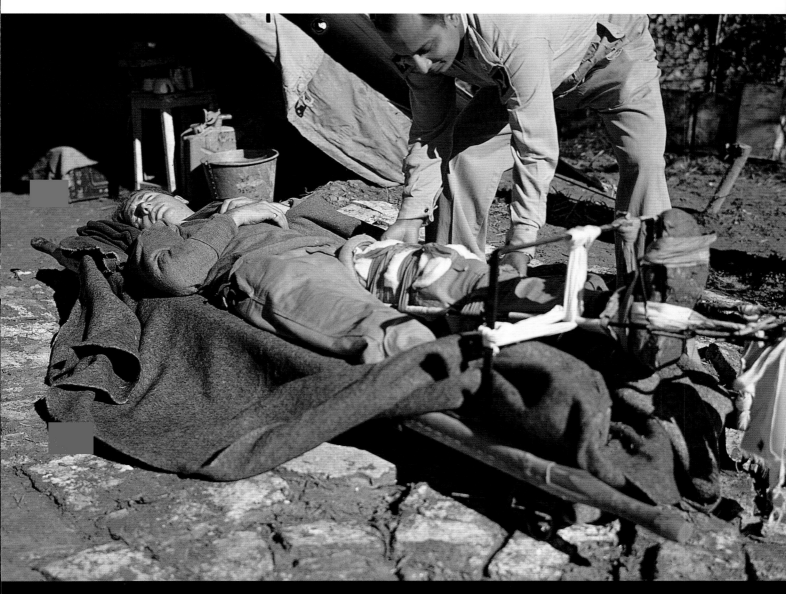

A SOLDIER'S WOUNDS ARE ASSESSED AT AN ADVANCED DRESSING STATION IN ITALY, OCTOBER, 1944.

came the dawn – and with it a lull while both sides sorted themselves out and had breakfast. While we were enjoying our bacon and beans, one of the chaps remarked "there isn't half a gun opened up and tore up the path within a couple of yards of us – we didn't laugh just at that moment, but it wasn't long before we saw the funny side.

We passed the 2 Div Memorial at KOHIMA on the way down and the inscription was, I thought, most touching, (please don't think me morbid) but it read

"When you go home tell them of us and say, For your tomorrow, we gave our today".

Well Dear I do so hope that I have made this little note interesting, and now I just must close, so for now I send you both my kindest regards and trust that soon, for you, the tumult and the shouting will have died, and for myself that it won't be along before this end of the globe follows suit. Remember me to all who know me and give them my love,

Yours most sincerely, George.

FEBRUARY 21 – APRIL 9, 1945
– MAJOR PETER GADSDON

Major Gadsdon served as a company commander with the 4th Battalion, 14th Punjab Regiment, during the Burma campaign. In 1945, he received the Military Cross for his leadership in the action at Letse.

FEBRUARY 21, 1945

Dear Mum and Dad

Have got half an hour in which to send you a line before we are off again. Have been in rather a bloody action this week, succeeded in capturing a town and killing off quite a lot of Japanese. Most unfortunately, our only remaining MC was killed. I am now commanding two companies for a time, and

MARCH 1945: BRITISH TROOPS REST IN FRONT OF ONE OF THE MANY COLOURFUL BUDDHAS ON PAGODA HILL, BURMA.

keeping my fingers crossed.

One or two incidents show what amazing creatures these Japs are. At one place I was facing them across about 300 yards of water – a lot of refugees were coming in, and one told me that there were two Japs watching me from a trench dug in the open right on the river bank. I really didn't believe him as it was an extraordinarily exposed position, but I turned on two mortars and trained a section of machine guns. The 6th round landed plonk on the trench and out they came! What a rabbit shoot! All my chaps let fly everything they had, and there were two less.

The people next door to us also report them still blowing themselves up with grenades rather than be captured. The old story.

I am wondering what this outfit is going to do now, with the Americans banging away at Tokyo. I suppose they know they have a long walk ahead of them, and no chance of getting away by sea. Of course, they are not fighting like the Kokima-Imphal days, but still have a bit of kick left.

I forgot to say that after I sprang their OP they were very quick with their little gun and got a direct on the building over my head! Very trying. Particularly as the thing was made of brick and mud and the wall bulged mightily. I hastily moved my HQ to another spot!

Cheerio! Must be off for the next round!

Lots of love Peter

MARCH 21, 1945

Dear Mum and Dad

News is of ten Japs, and one of my men, wounded and lying out in the open. Off I go at the double, get the rest of my outfit, and working round the enemy flank, put in a charge. Ten Japs! Hells bells, we were in a hornets nest of nearly a hundred! Up starts a machine gun, over go a coupleof my chaps and there we are with our faces in the dust, and a long crawl not assisted by the machine gun crackling overhead! We plastered them with artillery, and roared in again, to find one machine gun still firing. It was at this juncture that I bagged one myself – a standing shot at a Jap in a trench at about 75 yards. Got him slick through the head.

They had by then had enough, and with their usual conventions, came out and charged us! Not once, but twice! Just what we had been waiting for. We laid out 16 neat rows.

That fixed it – about 40 got up and ran like blazes straight into the people I had put to catch 'em. They killed 10.

After that the war died down, and I was able to collect my wounded, although there were still some Japs about the area. Altogether a good days rabbit shooting, as we were able to claim that we had put paid to 50 Japs.

We are all hopeful that we have taught the Jap a lesson over which he will ponder for a few days. I don't know what the final count is up there, but we have put a fair size force out of action.

I am fit, but it gets damn hot to play these games now.

Love Peter

APRIL 9, 1945

Dear Mum and Dad

It is queer that among your most recent

letters received was one telling me to eschew the medals and er – "keep my head down", so to speak. Sorry to disobey, but I am sure that you will be pleased to hear that I have been awarded the Military Cross. Your youngest son has not proved a disgrace to you.

It is however damned hot! Nothing else describes it. It is so damn hot that the old brain ceases to function. We get an hour a day cool – half past five to six in the morning and half past six to seven at night. The rest of the day is spent roaming miserably around in search of shade. Difficult to find on a bare hill full of trenches, where a dug-out acts as an oven!!

Still, we are winning, so what the hell! I listen assiduously to the wireless news every morning and watch the red pencil marks on my map of Germany heading across for Berlin in a steady march. The other day the Russians appeared in the bottom right hand corner round Vienna, so I am just waiting to hear the bugle blow the Stand Fast!

Lots of love Peter

MAY 1945, VE DAY – MRS M. DINEEN

In May 1945, the war in Europe was over, but rather than feeling excited, Mrs Dineen is overwhelmed.

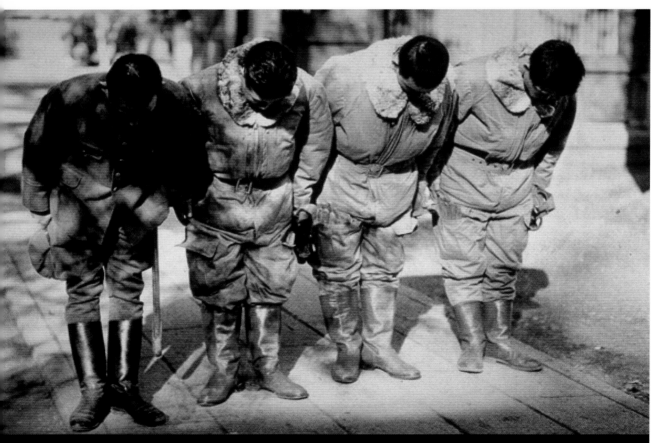

A GROUP OF "KAMIKAZE" PILOTS BOWING BEFORE THEIR MISSION, 1945. "SUICIDE" ATTACKS CONTINUED RIGHT UP UNTIL THE LAST DAYS OF WORLD WAR II.

And so Victory day has come. How do we all feel? I can only speak for myself. I don't feel excited. Perhaps the news of the last three days has been too much for me. To fully realize that London is safe and will no more be bombed, that we can return to our homes and that the war in Europe is over is more than we can truly understand. I think, to be truthful, I feel dazed. So much has come about and so much has to be done, I feel overpowered.

MAY 1945 – MRS M. DINEEN

With the end of the war, Mrs Dineen finds it hard to leave her new friends and busy life in Wales and to return home.

I began to feel lonely. I was alone from 8.20 until 5 p.m... I longed for the friendliness of the village folks and when letters came from the children still in Wales I just had to shed tears... My house is small so when the workmen had gone and everything was clean and tidy again I found I really didn't have enough to do all day...after having every moment filled for the past 6 years I didn't enjoy being idle. I thought and thought of my friends in Wales and many times wished I could have a chat with them.

MAY 1, 1945 – C. BAGGS

Private Gunner Corporal Baggs is liberated from his POW camp by US forces.

Day of Liberation

All morning we are watching the ridge about 2,000 yards away, expecting to see the Yanks come over. Hour after hour we wait, can you imagine our feelings, we are really excited. Just imagine after all these years, expecting relief, it's great.

Look, look, they're here, everyone nearly speechless and sure enough at 3pm "the good old Yanks" come. We all run out now and embrace our liberators, oh boy. What a feeling. Tears were plentiful. We now have a snap taken with a Yankee officer, who is beaming all over with pride. We round up the Jerries now disarm them put them together in a room. Once done, we go to town, all the cattle here, cows, pigs, hens are all shot, and we have 2 lads here who can skin and dress them, so no we can have what we fancy. The German farmer with his wife, are moved out into to pigs shed and I along with the Yankee sergeant take over bed etc, this is great, we put the wireless on, on windowsill and all the boys gather round with smiling faces now.

MAY 4, 1945 – C. BAGGS

Woke up at 3am and off again to Drome, would we get away this day? We hope to. At last we see about 30 Lancaster bombers coming, so now our hopes are high, sure enough 10:45am we are put into the bomber. Life belts as well and off we go for dear old Blighty. What a trip. I will never forget it, it nearly finished me, but we landed ok outside Oxford and what a fine reception, everything one needed, but really I was too ill, couldn't even like drink tea.

Then we were examined, x-rayed, and all our old clothes dumped, we were rigged out with everything new and felt a new man. Concert for us tonight and didn't we enjoy it. This is the life, plenty to eat, and no worries. Everyone looks will in their new rig-out and looking far happier than they have done for years.

MAY 8, 1945 – JACK CLARK

A member of the 143 Field Regiment, Royal Artillery, Jack Clark writes to his wife, conveying the VE Day emotions in occupied Germany.

8TH MAY 1945
2058212 Clark J
B Troop 190 Bty, 143 Field Reg. RA, B.L.A.

My Own Darling Olive,

Wasn't it wonderful news darling? In fact it

MARJORIE CHOWN MAKES GLASS EYES AT THE MINISTRY OF PENSIONS' BUILDING IN 1943.

seems all too good to be true. Today – VE Day – is the day we have been waiting for, but even so it doesn't seem possible somehow that we have at last won our War. I suppose you were tremendously excited and happy when you heard the news at home but it's hard to explain really and it may sound funny but it didn't somehow make much impression on us when we first heard the capitulation. It didn't seem to make a lot of difference at first. It was an English speaking civilian who came and told us and he must have thought us a pretty poor lot because, we didn't take much notice but just went on cleaning our Carrier! Later on in the evening we went over to the Gun Position and did a bit of celebrating. For this purpose we dug out our rum Bottle and drank the contents between the four of us and a double ration which was issued to mark the occasion as well! Outside all around and as far as you could see the sky was full of light, parachute flares, and illuminating flares of all colours. There were lines of tracer bullets and bofors shells streaming across the sky and in fact it was a real Guy Fawkes night.

After this we had to spit and polish everything in preparation for the big march forward. Whilst we were waiting yesterday morning to move off dressed in our Sunday best with all the vehicles shining and our webbing scrubbed white we received the news from Regimental Headquarters that all resistance everywhere had ceased. Our job is to go on into Holland and round up and disarm the Germans mostly S.S. troops and send them back to Germany. We started yesterday midday and came into the German lines about 25 miles. All along the roads the civilians were lined up cheering and waving flags and wearing orange shirts and ties and the girls orange dresses and ribbons and painted on the trees and walls were big slogans "Welcome" and "We Thank You".

On the wireless this morning we heard the official announcement of VE Day and that everyone, all over the world was celebrating it. We had no opportunity of celebrating at all and nothing to celebrate with literally not even water because the water supply has been off all day and only just come on again. Out here we always said that when Victory came the only people who would have the opportunity of celebrating would be those who did no fighting but I suppose that's just hard luck and we don't begrudge anyone who feels happy and has a good time these days.

Now it is evening and the sun is just going gown – Darling this would be such a wonderful place to go walking with you just you and I together with no more worries and fears for each other.

Sleep Well Darling and God Bless you and bring quickly the moment when we shall by lying together in each others arms once again for I love you and long for your Love to the very depths of my heart.

TUESDAY 8 MAY, 1945
– MISS HELENA MOTT
Miss Helena Mott, aged 73, has mixed feelings regarding the end of war.

I am sorry it is dull for those who wish to spend

A MEMBER OF THE ROYAL ARMY ORDNANCE CORPS HELPS CHOOSE A TIE FOR A SOLDIER ABOUT TO BE "DEMOBBED".

this day in rejoicing. We are thankful that in Europe heavy death lists will ease, but many yet, due to treachery on the enemy's part, will die on the eve of returning home – and in some pockets, fighting will still be severe as in Prague. I am thankful the Channel Isles are free. Though hardships will cease, unfortunately and actually there is but little to rejoice over. Europe is a shambles, starvation stares it and us in the face and all the wrong people will again take positions of trust – promises will fade into the mist of ineptitude and one will be able to point to this war as the greatest tragedy and travesty of all time. Great things have been done, heroic sacrifices made, men have spent themselves, for what? Rebuilding the ghastly ruins in time for the next break out and death of humanity and faith. Faith has needed much bolstering in this war, it will be stone dead in the next.

AUGUST 15, VJ DAY
– MRS NOELLE WILLIAMS

I wake up earlier than usual at 8am, hear the repeat of the PM's speech announcing defeat of Japan. It didn't seem to "touch" me last night but this morning I can't stop myself crying. It is all so wonderful to think that our brothers, relations, friends will all be alive next week instead of not knowing from day to day what is going to happen to them! And our prisoners – those who have had the hardest lot to bear in this war in my opinion. Only today I saw in the "On Active Service" column of the *Telegraph* that

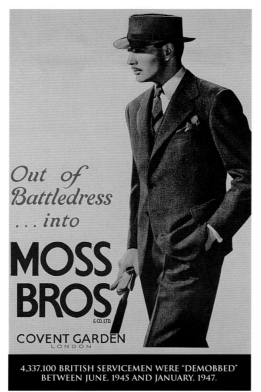

Out of Battledress ... into

MOSS BROS & CO. LTD.

COVENT GARDEN
LONDON

4,337,100 BRITISH SERVICEMEN WERE "DEMOBBED" BETWEEN JUNE, 1945 AND JANUARY, 1947.

some Cpl had died of starvation whilst in Japanese hands – poor devils, how thrilled and overjoyed they must be and their womenfolk at home who have had to live on hope for the last five years. It is indeed a great day for them. How we hope and pray that all their loved ones will be speedily restored to them...

The roads were very crowded till I got up to town. Going down Oxford St, I ran into a paper storm – torn up telephone directories being dropped from the rooftops on to the crowds below... The Americans from the Rainbow Club were on the balcony with a band and we all sang lustily "Tipperary", again made me weep a bit...a tidal wave of people would surge ahead and either push you backwards or forwards – you couldn't help yourself but just had to go with the crowd...

Trafalgar Square has a band playing with loud speakers...how happy everyone looks and all are wearing favours of some sort – Red, White and Blue flowers, ribbon, bows etc. Some very fancy hats I saw – three girls wearing Nell Gwynne hats, others little cardboard hats with "Kiss me quick", "Squeeze me tight" or "Get up them stairs" painted across them...quite clearly I can see a sea of heads stretching right down across Whitehall, up towards the Haymarket, a steady stream of people marching their way through Admiralty Arch to the Palace...

The few cars in The Mall hoot in vain – no one takes the slightest notice except to jump on the bumpers for a free ride... All around the palace was a sea of heads. The sun was shining and the Royal Standard flying well in a stiffish breeze. The balcony is draped with a dark red velvet or plush canopy with a long yellow fringe. Just as I am pushing my way into the crowd, a roar goes up, the balcony doors are beginning to open and the crowd calls for the King with renewed energy.

Near me I can see a jeep which is quite stuck in the crowd and hasn't a hope of moving up. Quickly hop onto the bonnet and have a marvellous view of their Majesties and the Princesses. The Queen in very pale blue with the same halo hat that she always wears, the King in the uniform of the Admiral of the Fleet, Princess Elizabeth I think in a fawn and yellow shade and Princess Margaret in blue. They all bow and acknowledge our cheers. Below me are masses of waving hands, squeakers, rattles, anything, all being waved at their Majesties. We all cheer and wave as loud as ever we can and I can't remember when I shouted so loud yet I can hardly hear my own voice _ it is just lost in the echoing cheers from about 100,000 people.

THURSDAY 16 AUGUST, 1945
– MRS A. LEE MICHELL
Mrs Lee Michell was a young married woman living in Somerset who had very mixed feelings about the end of the war.

Well, here ends the war and my diary – just a concluding note on our condition at the moment. All happy and joyful because of the war being over, and looking forward to getting our P.O.W.s back from Japan. But our larders are very bare & there are no houses for the returning soldiers to live in. And many of 'em are coming back to find small unwelcome black or American babies in their families – not so good. Workhouses and nursery schools crowded with the little bastards, and a wave of crime is sweeping Wellington. Boy of 16 has been forging cheques, a young soldier's wife has murdered her baby (not his) etc etc. Everyone's house needs painting & plastering, our clothes are getting very shabby and you can't buy a sheet or a blanket unless you have been newly-wedded & bombed out. Army is being de-mobbed bit by bit, we are up to date. Everyone full of hope about the Labour Government (Parliament opened on Tuesday) & among the blessings promised are national-ization of the Bank of England, Coal and elec-tricity, & a Minister for Housing. But already they are saying that it will all take time and meanwhile the miners are told they must dig more coal, and the M. of Housing is to be the M. of Workers for the present. So really there is no change at all. Life is going to be every bit as strenuous & the best minute of the day is just to sit down for a moment, however this doesn't often happen!

DECEMBER 11, 1945 – CYRIL CHARTERS
Cyril Charters arrived in France in June 1944. He was a projectionist with 37 Kinema Section RAOC and wrote extensively to his wife on the situation across northern Europe as he advanced towards Berlin.

Hello Darling,

I wonder how many people stop to think what life in Germany today is like. I wonder if they did think if they could picture what it really is like. It would be very hard. So here, to help that mental picture, I intend to give some idea of what

Germany and German people are today.

Berlin, where the stench of death and sewerage still pollutes the air, where water is disease infested, and gas and electricity non-existent, once the capital of Germany now so devastated that many experts declare that it can never be rebuilt. And where are the citizens of these dead cities? You will find them living in caravans and packed like sardines in country cottages. You know what the housing problem in England is like and you may guess, then, the condition over here.

Food is so scarce and extortionate prices are paid for Black Market. I know a driver who was given 30 silver Marks for a ting of bully beef (a silver Mark is valued at 2/-). In Berlin, the few remaining civilians clamour to buy cigarettes at 5/- a cigarette, – £2.10 – for a packet of Park Drive! It is not hard to see that cigarettes are more valuable than money, and that barter replaces buying things. Matches, too, are almost unobtainable and chocolate priceless. Money is useless and the Germans use their valuables (watches, jewellery) for purchasing goods.

To look in the shop windows is a waste of time; they are quite empty and usually boarded. We may guess what has happened to their goods. Buried first to prevent looking by the invading troops, they are now being used in exchange for foods and the needs of life.

Throughout Germany roam thousands of homeless refugees. Mingling with them are the de-mobbed members of the German Army, for the most part old men, making their own way home – on to where their homes once stood. And everywhere is the pathetic evidence of the cost of a man's ambition – hospitals filled to capacity with limbless men. Many villages are in reality little less than gigantic hospitals.

What have these people to live for? Their dear ones killed, their houses destroyed, tragedy and pathos everywhere around them, life is very bare. They thought to rule the world – all the agony, the tears and the suffering have recoiled on them a hundred fold. The Black Market they forced on other countries is now their own source of life, but worse, much worse.

Now cheerio again, sweet.

Your ever loving husband

Cyril xxx

CHRISTMAS 1945 – MRS M. DINEEN

By Christmas 1945, Mrs Dineen has settled back into her old life and is looking forward to building a new world.

The Victory Xmas of 1945 is a time of Thanksgiving. After almost six years of terrible war we are back home safe and sound. How many are united with their families and how many have homes to live in? Not many. There is still trouble in various places in the world and there will be until the people of Europe have food and warmth and a new idea of life, but we thank God with all our hearts that we three are together in our home after years of separation and we look forward to 1946 and the future with a smile and a grateful heart and hope to contribute in some small way to the building of a new world fit at last for our children to work in.

And so my diary ends.

TROOPS PASSING UNDER ADMIRALTY ARCH DURING THE VICTORY PARADE IN LONDON, 1946.

AUGUST 17, 1943: AN 8TH ARMY SOLDIER AND SICILIAN GIRL ENJOY THEMSELVES AFTER SICILY WAS CAPTURED BY THE ALLIES.

CHRONOLOGY

— 1935 —

WORLD EVENTS

January 13	91% of voters in the Saarland vote for incorporation into Germany.
February 22	Italian troops depart for East Africa.
March 1	Saarland is restored to Germany.
March 16	Germany introduces conscription and rejects the disarmament requirements of the Treaty of Versailles.
September 15	Hitler announces anti-semitic Nuremberg Laws at the Nuremberg Rally. They forbid marriage between Jews and Aryans, and sexual intercourse between them. They also make the Swastika the official German flag.
October 3	Italy invades Ethiopia.

BRITISH POLITICS

January	Cotton workers vote for a reduction in their industrial capacity. Former Prime Minister David Lloyd George advocates a statutory council to prepare economic development. It's called the New Deal.
May	Britain announces a major expansion of the RAF.
June	Stanley Baldwin becomes Prime Minister replacing Ramsay Macdonald and forms a new National Government.
June	A "peace ballot" records 11.6 million voters in favour of Support for the League of Nations.
July	After a mass meeting at the Albert Hall, London, the Peace Pledge Union is formed to oppose rearmament and the resort to war.
October	Clement Attlee becomes leader of the Labour Party when George Lansbury resigns because he is unable to support his party's decision to agree to the use of force against Italy.
November	The General Election results return the National Government:

CONSERVATIVES	388	LIBERAL	21
NATIONAL LIBERAL	33	LABOUR INDEPENDENT	154
NATIONAL LABOUR	8	LABOUR	4
		COMMUNIST	1
		OTHERS	4
	429		184

| November | Clement Attlee defeats Herbert Morrison and Arthur Greenwood in a vote for the Labour leadership. |
| December | After criticism of the Hoare-Laval Pact between Britain and France, Anthony Eden succeeds Samuel Hoare as British Foreign Minister. |

OTHER NEWS & EVENTS

- A 30 mph speed limit is introduced in built-up areas.
- The Green Belt is introduced to curb growing development around London.
- 35 mm "kodachrome" colour film is introduced by Eastman Kodak.
- British physicist Robert Watson-Watt develops the first "radar" equipment.
- George Gershwin writes Porgy and Bess.
- The first recordings are made of Victor Silvester's dance orchestra.
- Arsenal win the English football championship for the third year running.
- Barham wins racing's Triple Crown for the first time since 1903.
- The following films are released in 1935: Anna Karenina (Garbo), The Bride of Frankenstein (Karloff), David Copperfield (Dir. Selznick), A Night at the Opera (Marx Brothers), The 39 Steps (Dir. Hitchcock).

──────────── 1 9 3 6 ────────────

WORLD EVENTS

January 22	French Prime Minister Pierre Laval resigns following criticism of the Hoare-Laval Pact with Britain.
February 16	A coalition of left-wing parties wins in Spanish elections.
February 26	In a military rebellion in Japan three government ministers are murdered by junior officers. The Prime Minister resigns.
March 7	German troops occupy the Rhineland, against the stipulations of the Treaty of Versailles.
May 5	Italian troops enter Addis Ababa, ending the war in Ethiopia.
June 4	French socialist, Leon Blum, forms Popular Front government in France.
July 17	The Spanish army mutinies in Spanish Morocco, led by Francisco Franco. Mutinies throughout Spain follow, leading to the Spanish Civil War.
August 24	Germany adopts compulsory two-year military service.
November 3	President Roosevelt is re-elected for a second term in the United States.
November 18	Germany and Italy recognize Franco's government in Spain.

BRITISH POLITICS

January	Upon the death of King George V, Edward VIII accedes to the throne.
March	British defence spending increases dramatically from £122 million to £158 million.
June	Clement Attlee, Leader of the Opposition moves a censure motion against

	Baldwin's government over weak foreign policy (defeated by 384 to 170).
July	"Means-test" measures are introduced into British social policy.
October	200 men march from Jarrow to London to protest at high unemployment.
October	Oswald Mosley, leader of the British Union of Fascists, leads an anti-Jewish march along the Mile End Road in London's East End.
November	Edward VIII announces in private that he plans to marry Mrs Wallis Simpson, an American divorcee.
December	The King abdicates. The Duke of York becomes George VI. Edward VIII becomes the Duke of Windsor.

OTHER NEWS & EVENTS

– Billy Butlin opens his first holiday camp at Skegness.
– British aviator Amy Johnson flies to Cape Town. The journey takes just over three days.
– Prokofiev writes Peter and the Wolf.
– Margaret Mitchell writes Gone with the Wind.
– The Crystal Palace at Sydenham in London is burned to the ground.
– The Games of the 11th Olympiad are held in Berlin. Hitler uses them as a propaganda showcase. Germany win 33 gold medals.
– High-quality television begins in broadcasts by the BBC.
– The films of 1936 include: The Charge of the Light Brigade (Flynn), Flash Gordon (Crabbe), Modern Times (Chaplin), Things to Come (Prod. Korda), Mr Deeds Goes to Town (Dir. Capra).

— 1937 —

WORLD EVENTS

April 19	Spain's two main right-wing parties, the Falange and the Traditionalists, merge to form the Falange Española Tradicionalista.
April 27	Airplanes from the German Condor Legion bomb Guernica during the Spanish Civil War.
May 6	The Hindenburg, the German airship, explodes at Lakehurst, New Jersey, killing 36 people.
July 31	Japanese forces seize Beijing in the Sino-Japanese War.
August 9	The Japanese make a sea-borne assault on Shanghai.
December 13	Japanese troops capture Nanking. The Rape of Nanking ensues, in which over 250,000 Chinese are killed.

BRITISH POLITICS

January	The Public Order Act is introduced. Political uniforms are banned. Police are permitted to ban marches if disorder threatens.
January	British Communists, the Independent Labour Party and the Socialist League

	form the Unity campaign to oppose rearmament.
May	The coronation of King George VI takes place at Westminster Abbey.
May	Stanley Baldwin's retirement leads to Neville Chamberlain forming a new National Government. Anthony Eden is Foreign Secretary.
June	The Duke of Windsor marries Wallis Simpson in France.
September	The National Council of Labour supports Britain's role in the League of Nations and states that another war in Europe is not inevitable.
November	The Air Raid Precautions bill is introduced in the House of Commons.
November	Lord Halifax flies to see Hitler to assess German intentions in Europe, including issues like the Sudetenland Germans in Czechoslovakia.
December	The Leader of the Labour Party, Clement Attlee, visits Spain to support the Republican cause.

OTHER NEWS AND EVENTS

- The Matrimonial Causes Act equalizes the position of women in divorce proceedings in England and Wales.
- George Orwell writes The Road to Wigan Pier.
- Karen Blixen writes Out of Africa.
- Carl Orff writes Carmina Burana.
- John Steinbeck writes Of Mice and Men.
- Joe Louis wins the World Heavyweight boxing title by beating James J. Braddock in Chicago.
- The films of 1937 include: Camille (Garbo), Fire Over England (Dir. Howard), La Grande Illusion (Dir. Renoir), The Prisoner of Zenda (Prod. Selznick), Snow White and The Seven Dwarfs (Prod. Disney).

—————— 1938 ——————

WORLD EVENTS

February 4	Hitler declares that he will become commander of the German armed forces with General Keitel as Chief of Staff.
March 11	Anschluss: German troops march into Austria.
April 10	Edouard Daladier, a Radical Socialist, forms a new French government.
September 15	Chamberlain visits Hitler at Berchtesgaden. But Hitler reiterates his intention to annexe the Sudetenland.
September 18	Britain and France propose that Czechoslovakia accept Hitler's claim to the Sudetenland. The proposal is rejected.
September 22	On Chamberlain's second visit to Hitler, the German Chancellor proposes a military occupation of the Sudetenland by October 1.
September 29	At the Munich Conference Chamberlain and Daladier agree to German

military occupation of the Sudetenland in exchange for a guarantee of the rest of Czechoslovakia's borders. Chamberlain returns to London saying that he has brought back, "peace with honour...peace in our time".

October 1   Germany occupies the Sudetenland.

November 2   Japan withdraws from the League of Nations specialized agencies.

November 9   Kristallnacht (Crystal Night), in which Jewish homes, shops and synagogues are vandalized, burned and looted throughout Germany.

December 23   The Nationalists begin their attack on Catalonia in the Spanish Civil War.

BRITISH POLITICS

February   Anthony Eden resigns as Foreign Secretary in protest at Neville Chamberlain's policy on foreign affairs. Lord Halifax succeeds him.

February   Winston Churchill leads a parliamentary outburst against Chamberlain's policies.

October   The First Lord of the Admiralty, Alfred Duff Cooper, resigns in protest at the Munich agreement.

December   The National Register for War Service is established.

OTHER NEWS & EVENTS

- The Spens Report on English education recommends grammar, technical and modern schools for secondary education.
- Werner von Braun becomes director of the German rocket research centre at Peenemunde.
- Glenn Miller forms his second band.
- Graham Greene writes Brighton Rock.
- George Orwell writes Homage to Catalonia.
- Henry Armstrong becomes the first boxer to hold three world titles at different weights: featherweight, welterweight and lightweight.
- Italy retain the football World Cup during the third international tournament, held in France. They beat Hungary 4:2 in the final.
- Len Hutton scores a new test record of 364 as England amass a total of 903 for 7 declared against Australia at the Oval.
- Donald Budge wins the tennis Grand Slam.
- Orson Welles causes panic in a radio play broadcast on CBS, by announcing a Martian invasion of earth.
- The films of 1938 include: The Adventures of Robin Hood (Flynn), Alexander Nevsky (Dir. Eisenstein), Angels with Dirty Faces (Cagney), The Lady Vanishes (Dir. Hitchcock).

WORLD EVENTS

January 26	In the Spanish Civil War, the Nationalists take Barcelona.
February 27	Britain and France recognize Franco's Government in Spain.
March 15	German troops occupy Bohemia and Moravia and enter Prague. Slovakia becomes a Protectorate.
March 19	The French Prime Minister, Daladier, is given extensive power to re-arm and mobilize.
March 28	Madrid surrenders to the Nationalists. The Spanish Civil War ends with the surrender of the remaining Republican strongholds.
March 31	Britain and France promise to support Polish independence.
April 7	Italy invades Albania.
May 8	Spain leaves the League of Nations.
August 23	In the Nazi-Soviet Pact, secret agreements include the partition of Poland and freedom of manoeuvre for the USSR in the Baltic.
September 1	Germany invades Poland.
September 3	Britain and France declare war on Germany.
September 17	The Soviet Union invades Poland from the East.
September 27	Warsaw surrenders. The major part of the Polish army surrenders the next day.
November 4	President Roosevelt signs the Cash and Carry bill, allowing Britain and France to purchase US weapons.
November 30	The USSR invades Finland.
December 14	The Soviet Union is expelled from the League of Nations.

BRITISH POLITICS

April	Conscription for the British army is introduced for men aged 20–21.
June	King George VI visits the United States and Canada.
July	Winston Churchill promotes an alliance with the Soviet Union.
August	Parliament passes the Emergency Powers bill. The government is able to maintain public safety and the war effort by order in council.
September	The evacuation of women and children begins.
September	The Ministry of Information is established.
September	The British National Service bill allows men aged 18 to 41 to be called up.
September	Chamberlain forms a war cabinet, which includes Churchill as First Lord of the Admiralty.
September	HMS Courageous is sunk by a U-boat.
September	Income tax is raised from 5 shillings and sixpence to 7 shillings and sixpence (25p to 37p).
October	HMS Royal Oak is sunk at Scapa Flow.
November	60,000 tons of merchant ships are sunk off the east coast by magnetic mines in a single week.

| December | After a long pursuit, the German battleship Graf Spee is scuttled off Montevideo following the Battle of the River Plate. |

OTHER NEWS & EVENTS

- John Cobb breaks the world land speed record at Bonneville Salt Flats Utah with a speed of 368.85 mph.
- Malcolm Campbell sets a water speed record of 141.7 mph.
- Albert Einstein writes to President Roosevelt about the potential of atomic power. Roosevelt responds by establishing the Advisory Committee on Uranium to increase research efforts.
- James Joyce completes Finnegan's Wake.
- Steinbeck writes The Grapes of Wrath.
- J.R. Tolkien writes The Hobbit.
- In the Fifth Test between England and South Africa at Durban, the game is declared a draw after 10 days of play.
- "It's That Man Again" begins on BBC radio with Tommy Handley .
- The films of 1939 include: The Adventures of Sherlock Holmes (Rathbone), Gone With The Wind (Leigh/Gable), The Hunchback of Notre Dame (Laughton), Stagecoach (Wayne), The Wizard of Oz (Garland), Wuthering Heights (Olivier/Oberon).

--- 1940 ---

WORLD EVENTS

March 3	Soviet troops capture Vyborg in the Finno-Russian War.
March 12	The Treaty of Moscow ends the Russo-Finnish war.
March 20	Daladier resigns as French Prime Minister, to be replaced by Paul Reynaud.
April 9	German forces invade Denmark and Norway.
May 10	Germany invades the Netherlands, Belgium and Luxembourg, and makes a strike in the Ardennes to outflank the bulk of the French army.
May 26	The evacuation of British and French troops from the beaches of Dunkirk begins.
June 10	The French Government leaves Paris as the Germans close in on the city.
June 14	The German army enters Paris.
June 16	Reynaud resigns as Premier of France. He is replaced by Marshal Pétain who negotiates an armistice with Germany which results in the Vichy Government.
July 10	German planes begin bombing English ports and Channel shipping.
August 23	Bombing raids begin on London.
September 7	The Blitz begins.
September 15	The Luftwaffe suffer heavy losses on what will become known as Battle of Britain day.

| September 17 | Hitler postpones his invasion plan for Britain. |
| November 5 | Roosevelt is re-elected as American president for a third term. |

BRITISH POLITICS

January	Winston Churchill urges an alliance with the neutral states of Europe before they fall prey to Hitler's plans.
January	Rationing is introduced for bacon, butter and sugar.
April	Lord Woolton is made minister for food.
April	British, Polish and French code-breakers at Bletchley Park crack the secret of the German "Enigma" coding machine for transmitting radio messages.
May	Lord Beaverbrook is made minister for aircraft production.
May	Chamberlain, under fire after the debacle of the Allied attack on Norway, resigns, to be replaced by Winston Churchill, who forms a coalition government which includes Clement Attlee and Ernest Bevin.
May	The Local Defence Volunteers is formed (changed to Home Guard in July).
May	Oswald Mosley, leader of the British Union of Fascists, is interned.
November	A heavy German raid on Coventry kills 568 people and destroys much of the city centre, including the cathedral.

OTHER NEWS & EVENTS

- Free milk is provided for British mothers and babies.
- The George Cross is instituted for acts of civilian bravery.
- The BBC launches "Sincerely Yours", starring Vera Lynn.
- Ernest Hemingway writes For Whom the Bell Tolls.
- Graham Greene writes The Power and the Glory.
- The Olympic Games, due to be staged in Tokyo, are cancelled.
- The films of 1940 include: Fantasia (Prod. Disney), The Great Dictator (Chaplin), Rebecca (Dir. Hitchcock), The Road to Singapore (Crosby/Hope), The Westerner (Dir. Wyler).

———————————————— 1941 ————————————————

WORLD EVENTS

January 6	President Roosevelt outlines the Lend-Lease programme, allowing for the sale, lease or lending of goods to help the Allies.
February 6	British forces advance across Libya and occupy Benghazi.
February 12	General Erwin Rommel takes command of German forces in North Africa.
March 11	Lend-Lease is finally signed by Congress.
April 6	German forces invade Yugoslavia and Greece.
April 13	Rommel attacks Tobruk.
May 20	Germany invades Crete.
June 22	Operation Barbarossa – the German invasion of the Soviet Union begins.

September 8	German forces reach Leningrad, but fall short of the city.
September 19	Kiev falls to the German advance.
October 8	The German army takes Orel, south of Moscow.
October 16	Odessa falls to the Germans. When they are within 50 miles of Moscow, the Soviet government leaves the city. Stalin remains.
October 24	Kharkov falls.
November 3	Kursk falls.
December 6	After two failed German attacks on Moscow, the Soviets mount a counter-attack. The Russian winter sets in with a vengeance.
December 7	The Japanese make a surprise attack on the US naval base at Pearl Harbor.
December 8	The US and Britain declare war on Japan. The Japanese go on to the offensive in Burma, Malaya and the Philippines.
December 11	Germany and Italy declare war on the United States.
December 16	German forces outside Moscow begin to retreat.
December 19	Hitler takes personal command of the campaign.

BRITISH POLITICS

March	Ernest Bevin's "Essential Work Order" allows him to send labour to wherever it is needed.
April	The standard rate of income tax is raised to 10 shillings in the pound (50p to the £1).
May	Rudolf Hess flies to Scotland in mysterious circumstances. An apparent peace mission fails and he is arrested.
May	In a heavy raid on London, the Chamber of the House of Commons is destroyed.
May	HMS Hood is sunk by the German battleship, Bismarck. Bismarck is then sunk, while trying to make safe harbour in Brest, by the Royal Navy.
November	The HMS Ark Royal is torpedoed off Gibraltar and sinks.
December	Heavy penalties are introduced for "black marketeers".
December	The National Service bill lowers the call-up age to 18, and makes women liable for national service between the ages 20 and 30.

OTHER NEWS & EVENTS

- The Manhattan Project to develop atomic weapons begins in Chicago and Los Angeles.
- Noel Coward writes Blithe Spirit.
- "Utility" clothing and furniture is introduced in Britain.
- The "Brains Trust" begins on BBC radio.
- The films of 1941 include: Citizen Kane (Welles), High Sierra (Bogart), How Green Was My Valley (Dir. Ford), The Maltese Falcon (Bogart/Bacall).

WORLD EVENTS

January 5	The Soviet winter offensive begins on all fronts.
January 11	Kuala Lumpur falls to the Japanese.
February 1	Vidkun Quisling is appointed Minister-President of Norway.
February 15	Called "the worst disaster in British history" by Winston Churchill, Singapore falls to Japan.
February 16	Japan devours more territory in the East Indies and goes on to bomb Darwin in Australia on February 19.
April 18	The German spring offensive begins in the Ukraine.
April 18	United States bombers attack Tokyo, dubbed the "Doolittle Raid".
April 23	The Luftwaffe attack historic British towns, called the "Baedecker Raids", named after the German tourist guidebooks.
May 4	The naval battle of the Coral Sea takes place between the US and Japanese navies.
May 30	The first British "1,000 bomber" raid takes place against Cologne.
June 4	In the Battle of Midway, four Japanese carriers are sunk.
July 23	The German army take Rostov and push on to the Caucasus.
August 7	The Americans take a vital airfield on Guadalcanal and halt the Japanese territorial advance in the Pacific.
August 19	Bernard Montgomery takes command of the Eighth Army in North Africa.
August 19	The vital battle for Stalingrad begins.
October 23	Montgomery launches the Battle of El Alamein.
November 8	Operation Torch, the landing of Allied forces in Morocco and Algeria, takes place.
November 11	The German army occupies Vichy France under orders from Hitler.
November 19	A Soviet attack around Stalingrad isolates the German army in the city.

BRITISH POLITICS

February	A Ministry devoted to Production is established within the government.
February	Clement Attlee becomes Deputy Prime Minister.
March	The Dig for Victory campaign is intensified.
July	A motion of no confidence in the government's "central direction of the war" is defeated in the House of Commons.
July	The Second Front in Europe Campaign attracts 50,000 people to a demonstration in Trafalgar Square.
November	Sir Stafford Cripps leaves the War Cabinet to be replaced by Herbert Morrison.
December	The Beveridge Plan, William Beveridge's Social Security and Allied Services is published.

——— 1943 ———

WORLD EVENTS

January 2	The German withdrawal from the Caucasus begins.
January 14–23	At the Casablanca Conference, Churchill and Roosevelt agree on the unconditional surrender of Germany and Japan.
January 31	Field Marshal von Paulus and the remains of his army surrender at Stalingrad. General Stecker surrenders his troops two days later.
February 8	Orde Wingate leads his "Chindits" behind enemy lines in Burma.
February 25	American and British bombers begin round-the-clock bombing of German cities.
April 19	The Warsaw Ghetto rises against German occupation. They hold out for nearly a month. 14,000 defenders die.
May 13	The German and Italian armies in Tunisia surrender.
July 5	The Germans attack the Kursk Salient, thus beginning the largest tank battle in history.
July 13	The attack on Kursk is called off by Hitler. It will signal the beginning of a constant retreat on the Eastern Front.
July 25	Victor Emanuel III, King of Italy, dismisses Mussolini as Prime Minister.
September 3	Italian forces surrender unconditionally.
September 12	German commandos release Mussolini from prison in the Abruzzi mountains.
October 1	British forces occupy Naples.
November 6	The Red Army occupies Kiev.

BRITISH POLITICS

February	The Common Wealth Party, led by Sir Richard Acland, does much better than expected in the Ashford by-election. It is a jolt for the government.
April	The Common Wealth Party wins the Eddisbury by-election.
May	Part-time work is made compulsory for women aged 18–45.
May	Compulsory arbitration is introduced in the coal industry.
September	Sir Kingsley Wood's death while Chancellor of the Exchequer leads to the appointment of Sir John Anderson.
October	Ballots for National Service boys to be allocated to the coal mines are introduced – the "Bevin boys".
November	Lord Woolton is appointed Minister for Reconstruction in the War Cabinet.
November	Oswald Mosley is released from internment on health grounds.

OTHER NEWS & EVENTS

– Women are admitted to the Amalgamated Engineering Union in Britain.

– Aaron Copeland writes, Fanfare for the Common Man.

– Oklahoma! is staged in New York.

– The Nuffield Foundation is formed with an endowment of £10 million from William Morris, Viscount Nuffield.

- Penicillin is used successfully against chronic diseases.
- Hermann Hesse writes The Glass Bead Game.
- Zoot suits are in fashion in the USA.
- The films of 1943 include: I Walked with a Zombie (Dir. Tourneur), Jane Eyre (Dir. Welles), Lassie Come Home (Lassie's debut, but as a male dog Pal).

─────────────── 1 9 4 4 ───────────────

WORLD EVENTS

January 22	British and American forces land at Anzio, Italy.
January 27	The Red Army lifts the siege of Leningrad.
March 4	US bombers begin daylight raids on Berlin.
May 11	A fourth attack on the strategic point of Monte Cassino, on the German Gustav Line, is finally successful.
June 4	Allied armies enter Rome.
June 6	Operation Overlord, the D-Day landings in Normandy, begins.
June 13	German V1 flying bomb attacks begin on mainland Britain.
June 15	US forces take Saipan in the Marianas.
July 3	The Red Army takes Minsk.
July 9	The Allies take Caen in northern France.
July 18	General Tojo resigns as Japanese Prime Minister following the loss of Saipan.
July 20	Hitler survives a bomb plot at his headquarters in East Prussia. The plotters are executed.
August 1	Warsaw: The Polish Home Army rises against the German occupiers. They fight on until October before their resistance is finally crushed, despite the presence of thousands of Soviet soldiers on the outskirts of the city.
August 15	Operation Dragoon sees the Allies land on the French Mediterranean coast.
August 26	Charles de Gaulle enters Paris in a triumphant procession along the Champs Elysées.
September 8	V2 rocket attacks begin against Britain.
September 11	US troops cross into German territory near Trier.
September 17	Airborne assaults on the Maas, Waal and Rhine lead to a major British set-back at Arnhem.
October 23–26	The Battle of Leyte Gulf in the Philippines leads to a decisive victory for the US fleet.
November 7	Roosevelt wins a fourth term in office.
November 24	B-29 bombers from Saipan make the first raids on Tokyo since the Doolittle Raid of 1942.
December 16	The German army launches an attack through the Ardennes – the Battle of the Bulge.

BRITISH POLITICS

January   The Common Wealth Party wins the Skipton by-election.
February   The South Wales Miners go on strike.
February   Pay-As-You-Earn income tax collection is introduced.
April   Aneurin Bevan campaigns for the end of ministerial powers to deal with strikes.
May   The Education Act, introduced by R.A. Butler the President of the
               Board of Education, introduces the 11+ examination, along with a
               whole range of educational reforms.

OTHER NEWS & EVENTS

– The future structure of the United Nations is decided at a conference at
  Dumbarton Oaks, Washington DC.
– The World Bank, the International Monetary Fund and a world economic system based
  on fixed exchange rates is decided at the Bretton Woods Conference in New Hampshire.
– Glenn Miller is killed in an air crash.
– Tennessee Williams writes The Glass Menagerie.
– The Olympic Games of 1944, due to be held in London, are cancelled.
– The films of 1944 include: Henry V (Olivier), Ivan the Terrible (Dir. Eisenstein),
  To Have and Have Not (Dir. Hawks).

--------------------------------- 1945 ---------------------------------

WORLD EVENTS

January 17   The Soviet army captures Warsaw.
January 27   Soviet forces liberate Auschwitz.
February 4   The Big Three – Stalin, Roosevelt and Churchill – meet at Potsdam. They
               agree to the division of Germany and a division of Korea at the 38th parallel.
February 13   The Allied bombing of Dresden leads to a firestorm and an estimated 60,000
               deaths. The German army surrenders in Budapest.
February 19   The US assault on the island of Iwo Jima begins.
March 20   British and Indian troops enter Mandalay in Burma.
April 1   US forces land on Okinawa.
April 12   President Roosevelt dies and is succeeded by Harry S. Truman.
April 28   Mussolini and his mistress are executed in Italy.
April 30   After marrying Eva Braun, Hitler commits suicide in his Berlin bunker.
May 2   The German army surrenders in Berlin.
May 8   Following the formal surrender of the German armed forces the day before,
               Victory in Europe is declared.
July 5   General MacArthur announces the Japanese defeat in the Philippines.
July 17   The Potsdam Conference takes place, attended by Stalin,
               Truman and Churchill; Attlee, Leader of the Opposition, accompanies

	Churchill as a British General Election is pending.
	Unconditional Japanese surrender is demanded.
August 6	The United States drops an atom bomb on the Japanese city of Hiroshima.
August 8	The Soviet Union declares war on Japan and invades Manchuria.
August 9	A second atomic weapon is dropped on the city of Nagasaki.
August 14	It is announced that the Japanese Emperor will formally accept the Allies' terms for ending the war.
August 24	President Truman orders the end of the Lend-Lease arrangements.
September 2	Japan signs the formal surrender aboard the USS Missouri in Tokyo Bay. The country is placed under the control of General MacArthur.
September 2	Ho Chi Minh declares independence for Vietnam.
October 9	Pierre Laval is sentenced to death for collaborating with the Germans.
October 11	Fighting breaks out in China between Chiang Kai-shek's Nationalists and Mao Zedong's Communists.
November 20	The Nuremberg War Crimes Tribunal opens.

BRITISH POLITICS

March	The Family Allowance is introduced.
April	The first female Metropolitan Police Court magistrate is appointed.
April	Geoffrey Fisher is enthroned as Archbishop of Canterbury in succession to Archbishop Temple.
June	The Greater London Plan is published, outlining areas of economic development and population densities for London.
July	Labour win the General Election with a landslide, winning 399 seats to the Conservatives 213. Attlee forms a new government.

OTHER NEWS & EVENTS

- The Arab League is founded in Cairo.
- The French Government nationalizes the Bank of France, Air France and the Renault car company.
- UNESCO, the United Nations Educational, Scientific and Cultural Organization is founded.
- Benjamin Britten writes Peter Grimes.
- Carousel (Rodgers and Hammerstein) is performed in New York.
- George Orwell writes Animal Farm.
- Jean-Paul Sartre writes The Age of Reason.
- Bebop sweeps America.
- Matt Busby is appointed manager of Manchester United football club.
- The films of 1945 include: Brief Encounter (Dir. David Lean), Les Enfants du Paradis (Carné), The Southerner (Renoir).

1946

January 10	A truce is declared in the Chinese Civil War.
January 30	The inaugural session of the United Nations opens in London.
March 5	Churchill delivers a speech at Fulton Missouri, saying that Stalin has lowered an "Iron Curtain" from the Baltic to the Adriatic and that he is determined to spread the gospel of communism. The speech marks the symbolic beginning of the Cold War.
April 27	French troops bombard Haiphong, killing thousands. This marks the beginning of the Indo-China War and, ultimately, the Vietnam War.

BRITISH POLITICS

February	The Trade Disputes Act, which had outlawed sympathy strikes, is repealed.
March	The Bank of England is nationalized.
May	The House of Commons votes for the nationalization of the coal mines.
November	A Royal Commission supports equal pay for women.
November	The bill to nationalize transport is introduced.

OTHER NEWS & EVENTS

- The International Court of Justice is opened at The Hague.
- US scientists win all the Nobel prizes.
- The first bikinis are modelled in Paris.
- 33 spectators are killed at Burnden Park, Bolton, when a wall collapses during a game between Bolton Wanderers and Stoke City.
- Sugar Ray Robinson wins the world welterweight title by beating Tommy Bell at Madison Square Garden in New York.
- The BBC begins broadcasting Alastair Cooke's "Letter from America".
- The films of 1946 include: La Belle et la Bête (Dir. Cocteau), The Best Years of Our Lives (Dir. Wyler), The Big Sleep (Dir. Hawks).

BIBLIOGRAPHY

Calder, Angus   *The People's War: Britain 1939–1945* (London, 1969)

Dear, I.C.B. (ed.)   *The Oxford Companion to the Second World War* (Oxford, 1955)

Donnelly, Mark   *Britain in the Second World War* (London, 1999)

Gilbert, Martin   *A History of the Twentieth Century, Vol II* (London, 1998)

Keegan, John   *The Second World War* (London, 1990)

Marwick, Arthur   *A History of the Modern British Isles 1914–1999* (Oxford, 2000)

Weinberg, Gerhard L   *A World at Arms: A Global History of World War II* (Cambridge, 1994)

Ziegler, Philip   *London at War 1939–1945* (London, 1998)

Zweiniger-Bargielowska, I   *Austerity in Britain 1939–1955* (Oxford, 2000)

INDEX

ACKNOWLEDGEMENTS

The authors are grateful to all those near and far, from the present and the past, who made *Britain at War in Colour* possible.

We are several and they are legion, but particular mention should be made of Trans World International, the excellent production company for which we work, Carlton, our partners, for their immense support and ITV, which commissioned both "Second World War in Colour" and "Britain at War in Colour".

Everyone on the production team at TWI is owed an immense debt of gratitude by us all.

Our thanks also go to our publishers at Carlton Books for producing such an outstanding product.

Finally, to everyone around us who make life enjoyable and successful, thank you.

PICTURE CREDITS

The publishers would like to thank the following sources for their kind permission to reproduce the pictures in this book:

AKG, London 81
Estate of Jeff Ethell 14, 19b, 30, 111, 122
Hulton Getty 1, 15, 16, 18, 20, 25, 33, 34, 38, 42t,b, 58, 61, 62, 67, 68, 70, 72br, 73, 77t, 85, 88b, 93, 109, 120, 132, 139
collections of the Photograph Archive at the Imperial War Museum, London 5, 6-7, 10, 22, 26, 43bl, 48, 53, 64t,b, 65t (TR37), 65b (TR9), 66b, 69 (TR1928), 71 (TR451), 75 (NOE4), 76 (TR968), 82 (TR517), 84b (TR318), 84t (TR330), 87 (TR1573), 88t, 89 (TR1838), 90(TR494), 92 (TR1004), 95 (TR90), 97 (TR1662), 103 (TR1206), 104 (TR2321), 112bl (TR2043), 114t (TR1643), 114b (TR1642), 115 (TR1646), 116 (TR1375), 119 (TR1840), 124 (TR1127), 129 (TR2406),
135 (TR1582), 136, 140 (TR1247)
Imperial War Museum, London/Rosie Newman 19t, 37, 47, 51, 52, 66t, 72tl, 77b, 113, 121, 123
Popperfoto 2, 8, 12, 23, 24, 40, 43tr, 44, 45, 57, 78, 79, 83, 86, 91, 94, 96, 98, 99, 100, 101, 102, 106t,b, 107, 108, 110, 112tr, 117, 118, 130, 134,

Every effort has been made to acknowledge correctly and contact the source and/or copyright holder of each picture, and Carlton Books Limited apologises for any unintentional errors or omissions which will be corrected in future editions of this book.